Andreas Treske
Video Theory

Media Studies

Andreas Treske is an author, filmmaker, and media artist living in Turkey. He graduated from the University of Television and Film, Munich, where he also taught film and video post-production. He teaches in the Department of Communication and Design at Bilkent University, Ankara, visual communication and media production, incl. new media. He is a member of the video vortex network and corresponding member of CILECT, the world association of film schools.

Andreas Treske
Video Theory
Online Video Aesthetics or the Afterlife of Video

[transcript]

Bibliographic information published by the Deutsche Nationalbibliothek
The Deutsche Nationalbibliothek lists this publication in the Deutsche Nationalbibliografie; detailed bibliographic data are available in the Internet at http://dnb.d-nb.de

© 2015 transcript Verlag, Bielefeld

All rights reserved. No part of this book may be reprinted or reproduced or utilized in any form or by any electronic, mechanical, or other means, now known or hereafter invented, including photocopying and recording, or in any information storage or retrieval system, without permission in writing from the publisher.

Cover layout: Kordula Röckenhaus, Bielefeld
Cover illustration: Andreas Treske, Jörn Fröhlich, Nigel Ashley, 2013, Izmir/Turkey. Copyright: Andreas Treske
English editor: Michael W. Phillips Jr.
Printed in Germany
Print-ISBN 978-3-8376-3058-9
PDF-ISBN 978-3-8394-3058-3

Shall I project a world?
THOMAS PYNCHON/THE CRYING OF LOT 49

Contents

ACKNOWLEDGEMENTS | 9

STATIC—OCEAN BLUE | 11

VIDEO UNCHAINED | 25

V-BRICKS | 71

TYRANNICAL LOOPS | 97

WAYS OF SEEING | 119

BEYONCE VERTICAL | 133

INTERIORS & EXTERIORS | 151

SPACE IS ONLY NOISE | 167

ILLUSTRATIONS | 187

BIBLIOGRAPHY | 189

ACKNOWLEDGEMENTS

This text wouldn't have come into existence without Geert Lovink and the VIDEO VORTEX project, its series of conferences, and its network of people concerned with ONLINE VIDEO.

Geert Lovink supported my writing from the earliest stages. He insistently motivated me to continue my research, for which I am more than thankful.

VIDEO VORTEX gave me a forum to formulate my vague ideas about video from my practice as filmmaker and teacher between cinema, TV and YouTube. I had the chance to participate in most of the Video Vortex events and also organized two events in Ankara and Istanbul to bring together an enriching community, fostering and questioning present phenomena, practices, discourses and theories of online video and digital culture.

Tom Sherman, Aras Özgün, and Andrew Clay were not only the first readers and critical reviewers of my texts, but also friends and mentors I am grateful to.

I would like to thank Vera Tollmann, Albert Figurt, Perry Bard, Özge Çelikaslan, Lewis Johnson, Ahmet Gürata, Serkan Şavk, Nezih Erdoğan, Oliver Lerone Schultz, Dan Oki, Jan Simons, Vito Campanelli, Natalie Bookchin, Stefan Heidenreich, Murat Karamüftuoğlu, Ranya Renee, Heike Henzmann, Ege Berensel, Federico Puletti, Jens Schroeter, Stephan Vorbrugg, Jürgen Kühnel, Zuhal Ulusoy and many, many more. A special note belongs to Geneviève Appleton for her on-going collaboration, helpfulness and willingness to stand by.

A very special thanks goes to Margreet Riphagen, Miriam Rasch, and Patricia de Vries from the Institute of Network Cultures in Amsterdam for their passion and engagement in our project.

And, of course, many, many thanks to Michael W. Phillips Jr. for editing this text.

Finally, I am greatly happy to thank Lale Gülden Treske for her love, energy and encouragement. I dedicate this book to her.

»To compose a finished, well-constructed poem, the mind is obliged to make projects that prefigure it. But for a simple poetic image, there is no project; a flicker of the soul is all that is needed.« (Bachelard 1994, xxii)

For Gülden

Ankara, January 2015

STATIC—OCEAN BLUE

> The sky above the port was the color of television, tuned to a dead channel.
> WILLIAM GIBSON/NEUROMANCER

> Static, static, static. Be static! Movement is static! Movement is static because it is the only immutable thing—the only certainty, the only thing that is unchangeable. The only certainty is that movement, change, and metamorphosis exists. That is why movement is static.
> JEAN TINGUELY/ZERO 3

FLOATING

BLUE. It is blue. The color of VIDEO is blue. A dead channel is black. Black is nothing. If a screen is black, then nothing is streamed, no content, no signal, and no function. Stand by? No, if the screen is black, then it is malfunctioning or defunct, or there is no reception. No signal, or no electricity, no connection, no network? It defines a lack, emptiness. There is something. And this something is nothing. Restart.

Blue is the screen when there is a connection identified, a technical signal transmitted and displayed, a lack of content, another emptiness, but defined and limited. There is something and that something is technical and operational, a framework unfilled. Simple On.

When the screen is not blue, it is colorful, a change of light, frequently. The screen is emitting light—bluish, technically, in reference to its color temperature. When video is playing/streaming, it lights up its surroundings, its environment with changing colors, brightness, contrast, intensities and densities.

I wonder what would be the color of all videos, played all together at the same time, streamed at once onto a huge screen looked at from a distance far, far away. Would it be blue like EARTH or would it be the color of TELEVISION referred to in the opening line of William Gibson's novel *Neuromancer*?

»The sky above the port was the color of television, tuned to a dead channel.« (Gibson 1984)

When Gibson's famous cyberpunk novel was published in 1984, the public imagination of a television sky would be a grayish sky constructed by a noisy disturbed analog signal, lots of random dots instead of blue. STATIC! It is something seen on analog television after transmission ends, when there was no signal, or at the end of analog videotape when there was no more recording.

Some people called it SNOW—TV SNOW.

The colors of all videos together I assume should mix to the color of their light source—technically, their illumination, 5000 Kelvin, the color temperature of the bluish light point, which is moving in time, creating a rapid succession of images defined in a specific aspect ratio.

If our visual perception were quick enough to trace the movement of the little light dot—the tiny beam—writing the image on the phosphorus layer on its back (or, "in the inside"), what would we see on the screen? What would we see on our devices? We would see a point changing its position in a grid, changing its brightness and color. There is no image in video, at least not a photographic one, where the light is frozen in a single instance.

All videos of this moment seen together I imagine rather would appear similar to the view of the Mediterranean Sea from a sandy beach close to the Turkish holiday resort Çeşme or from a ship on a blue cruise along the

Turkish Riviera—the look down to the bottom of the Mediterranean water clear and the colors changing to TURQUOISE. Fishes swimming.

It is calming. Without describing any single video, just thinking about the amount of video viewed all together, ignoring any single entity or form or video object, just meditating on the sum, finally a calm OCEAN appears. The ocean is wide and deep. It has no end. It is around us and we are in it—an ocean of video. We see blue, an eternal blue. »But in that last is the unexpected in the face of the eternal: Blue is the color that knows no boundaries, knows no answers, and asks no questions. Blue is the eternal, the loss of discrimination and hatred, the blue of heaven.« (Jurek n.d.)[1]

It is the sky above us, the never-ending sphere of dreams. The sum of all videos is the freedom unleashed from the chains of the single image. »It is the terrestrial paradise« (Jarman 1993).

STATIC—WAR OF THE ANTS

We are using the word *static* with lots of different meanings. Static could refer to a static electricity, the charge of an object; static could mean the effect appearing when shoes rub on a carpet; static could be the white noise, the random signal with a flat power spectral density, a random crackling in a radio receiver, produced by atmospheric disturbance of the signal. It could be a branch of physics concerned with physical systems in equilibrium, relating to bodies at rest or forces that balance each other, forces that

---

1   Blue was all the nearly blind painter and filmmaker Derek Jarman could see before his death and while making his remarkable last film with the same title. The 79-minute film *Blue* is shot entirely »of a blue background, with narrators giving voice to Jarman's fearless confrontation of sight loss and imminent mortality. It lists the effects of the virus [HIV], recounts the tedium of hospital visits and endless pill-popping, and recalls past lovers, living and lost. It may sound inaccessible, but it's an incredible sensory experience complemented by an immersive and beautiful score by Simon Fisher Turner and Brian Eno« (Davidson 2014).

do not produce movement; or it could be fluid statistics, static pressure, or static space-time.

Static in sociology refers to characteristic of or relating to a society that has reached a state of equilibrium so that no changes are taking place.

Of course, when television people or moviemakers refer to it, they talk about the snow seen on a television screen. It is not only them; all the human generations that lived analog television were clearly aware of the little random jumping white and black dots on the screen when there was no program broadcasted, when there was not a signal but just a "snowy" noise pattern.

Static was the first image experience when installing a new analog television set at home, and it was usually the last experience when the channel or the station finished its daily program, helping thousands of people sleep on the sofa. When in Europe in the 1980s broadcasters started to transmit 24 hours, for a while it became popular to fill the empty slot in the very early mornings with live footage from a fish tank or the front window of a train passing through the Bavarian landscape replacing the static.

Static results from electronic and electromagnetic noise picked up by the antenna. In digital broadcast, static is nearly nonexistent for the television audience; if static noise becomes visible, it is somehow less random and more still like another meaning of static—not moving or less moving, stationary or at rest. But most modern televisions automatically change to a blue screen and go to standby after some time if the only signal input present is static. The broadcast is resting, and so is the device.

Static in general is characterized as a lack of activity, a lack of change, of movement, or of progress. The noisy electromagnetic interference image disrupting the reception of television is clearly related to communications in an analog world. On the Internet and in computer programming, static elements are those that are fixed and incapable of any kind of action or change; they're the opposite of dynamic websites or programming. Dynamic programming therefore means to assign the capability of action and change.

»When a Web page is requested (by a computer user clicking a hyperlink or entering a URL), the server where the page is stored returns the HTML document to the user's computer and the browser displays it. On a static Web page, this is all that happens. The user may interact with the document through clicking available links, or a small program (an applet) may be activated, but the document has no capacity to return information that is not pre-formatted. On a dynamic Web page, the user can make requests (often through a form) for data contained in a database on the server.« (Rouse 2005)

Static, according to the Urban Dictionary, has much different qualities than the ones we've seen thus far:

Static causes friction during intense situations, and is an unnecessary contribution of verbal, physical, and/or emotional aggression.[2] »Static is the act of giving shit to boys when they aren't treatin the sistas propa, or the nickname for girlfriends lookin out for their sistas when the boys aren't acting propa.« (Urban Dictionary n.d.)

Statics is the beginning class for most civil and mechanical engineers, electric charge that is built up, something that's fresh, like attitude, or backtalk, also, resistance or reluctance.

Static can be said to be a paranoid behavior around police or any other authority.

Static is »The white and black flakey crap that comes up on your television when you don't get a certain channel« (Urban Dictionary n.d.).

Static is »being extraordinary. Inspirational. Electrifying. Stands out in a crowd. Completely misunderstood. Has extreme determination. Static is unable to be labeled. Undefined. Thrilling. Incredible vibe« (Urban Dictionary n.d.).

Static is a character in a book, which is not undergoing change. It is a »word used when someone either says or does something repetitively to the point where the action or phrase is getting annoying« (Urban Dictionary n.d.).

STATIC is also the name of a 2013 short film by Ege Ulucan based on a haiku by Shuson Kato:

---

2   From The Urban Dictionary a reference to Quentin Tarantino's film "Reservoir Dogs": »...Managers know better than to fuck around, so if you get one that's giving you static, he probably thinks he's a real cowboy, so you gotta break that son-of-a-bitch in two...«

»I kill an ant
and realize my three children
have been watching.« (Kato n.d.)

Ulucan uses parallel editing to combine footage of busy ants with detailed shot of brushing a stone floor with water to clean away the blood of sacrificed animals. The blood and water run into a sewer opening. When the movement of ants and cleaning becomes more intense through the action as well as through the selection of closer shots, she cuts to the image of static and the disturbance of a video signal. The image fades to black and the haiku appears on the screen (Ulucan 2013).

Static in this short student film functions as a dramatic, disturbing and disorienting element, but also as a quote. The disturbance and imbalance is portrayed through the shots of moving ants and the blood on the floor in the next shot. The parallel editing is interrupted by or culminates in the static, therefore duplicating and extending what Ulucan intended—the feeling of the observer with the camera in her hand. The quote is a double quote, first through the participation and documentation of ant life, their movement and activity, ants as the dots in the analogue static constantly moving; and second through cutting to the disturbed signal itself.

»Since one impression of the 'snow' is of fast-flickering black bugs on a cool white background, in Sweden, Denmark and Hungary the phenomenon is often called myrornas krig in Swedish, myrekrig in Danish, hangyák háborúja in Hungarian, and semut bertengkar in Indonesian, which translate to 'war of the ants' or sometimes hangyafoci which means 'ant soccer', and in Romanian, purici, which translates into 'fleas'.« (Wikipedia n.d.)

THE PLEASURES OF VIDEO

»Imagine someone (a kind of Monsieur Teste in reverse) who abolishes within himself all barriers, all classes, all exclusions, not by syncretism but by simple discard of that old specter: logical contradiction; who mixes every language, even those said to be incompatible; who silently accepts every charge of illogicality, of incongruity; who remains passive in the face of Socratic irony (leading the interlocutor to the supreme disgrace: self-contradiction) and legal terrorism (how much penal evidence is based on a psychology of consistency!). Such a man would be the mockery of our society: court, school, asylum, polite conversation would cast him out: who endures contradiction without shame? Now this anti-hero exists: he is the reader of the text at the moment he takes his pleasure. Thus the Biblical myth is reversed, the confusion of tongues is no longer a punishment, the subject gains access to bliss by the cohabitation of languages working *side by side*: the text of pleasure is a sanctioned Babel.« (Barthes 1975, 3)

If we replace the word *text* with the word *video*, the last passage of Barthes' text reads like this:

Now this anti-hero exists: he is the reader of the video at the moment he takes his pleasure. Thus the Biblical myth is reversed, the confusion of tongues is no longer a punishment, the subject gains access to bliss by the cohabitation of languages working side by side: the video of pleasure is a sanctioned Babel.

In the West, Babel stands for the ultimate punishment—after Babel, the tongues are split. What Barthes proposes provokes the Western tradition emphasizing contradiction and confusion. The confusion of languages is something positive, sensible, and full of pleasures.

The term *reader* might be still the accurate characterization and might not need to be changed to construct a meaningful conclusion, as it is not just a viewer watching a video or a user engaging with a video. A video is constructed like television by a reading and writing process. Viewer and user are readers and writers. As the reader becomes or became the writer, the viewer (who was once called audience) is the producer, the blogger, the author—also the activist, the gamer, the inventor, the hacker and more. Berthold Brecht has already described and demanded the transformation of the radio listener into the producer. A text is not only readable but also writable, a video viewable as well as editable.

Pleasure, on the one hand for Barthes, confirms the reader's expectations and establishes cultural conventions, but bliss, as a state of perfect happiness, euphoria, or joy on the other is unsettling and creates a crisis against our cultural assumptions. It is a step too far.

For A New Aesthetic

This is a text about video. Its aim is to think about video—or better, rethink video. Video has become such a daily element of our lives that we rarely reflect on it, the way we use it, when and how we use it, its forms and appearances. Video plays many different roles.

It is not only that we do not think or question what is this thing we call *video*; we also don't find it relevant to do so. Video is something of the everyday, like driving a car or taking a shower. It is with us and around us, available on demand and attached to objects, skins, structures and architectures in our environment, the locations, places, and spaces where we live. Video plays on remote or in our field of sight. Recording anything—any important event of our lives, a birthday party, a wedding, a car accident, a demonstration, a beautiful tourist site, some cats—is absolutely simple and readily available. It's also easy to modify a recorded video, trimming its head and tail, combining it with music, adjusting the color. The way we process video reflects our skills, and reflects our habits, our individual experiences. It also defines and states our emotions.

It is true that video through the Internet became something lifelike. Video became a life of its own. As a simple matter of fact, »we are conditioned by our context, our beliefs, histories, emotional dispositions, physical needs, and communities.«[3] Online video not only is an essential element of expression and relation to our conditions, but is acting with us. With the world around us constantly changing, video went beyond a simple practical expansion of television technology. Similar to how Ludwig Wittgenstein described language, the way we use video and continue using video further is a »form of life.«

---

3 In a rewriting of Wollheim and Wittgenstein we are conditioned by our context, our beliefs, histories, emotional dispositions, physical needs, and communities. The world we interpret is a world of constant change. For Wittgenstein, language is a 'form of life', because the way we use language is always a reflection of our individual experiences, habits, and skills. This points towards the many different roles language plays in our lives. See: *Wittgenstein and Wollheim: Seeing-As and Seeing-In* (2013), Cooper (1985, 443-453), Matteucci (2013).

Video goes beyond television and cinema, and thus we need a different set of conceptual tools to discuss it. If we continue to use the categories and tool sets based on established media theories developed out of practices defining cinema and television as the dominant media and cultural technologies, we will be unable to see and include the potential and multiple transformations of such an entity, form and experience. These existing tools condescend to video as a rising amateur culture, when actually in its developmental states, video frees the moving image from its architectural corset and employs device technologies to mobilize and reshape.

The beauty of video is that it is uncontrolled and unstructured; it does not underlie a system of narrative dictatorship. It is free of the television mode of control and elimination of worlds. It stands in opposition to the worlds of power and systems of social control and organization. Video is free from the complex and carefully designed structure of something wanting something—it is a mode of choice. Video is atmospheric. Video is constantly creating, modifying, and tinkering with new atmospheres of being and togetherness.

We are asked to formulate an aesthetic theory as a form of radical gesture, an aesthetics as a politics of form and experience that is honest and truthful, and to reflect upon a realness of multiple worlds and forms of living with these worlds in what has been reality.

In the fusion of culture, remix and mash, the ocean of video, is ignoring the constrictions of an established system of media, and its operations. It ignores the construction of televised society of elderly and wise men, of one person speaking to many others. An aesthetic theory of video, reflecting on a manifestation of video as life and thought, and acknowledging videos dual character as either form or object or frequency or wave of events calls in its various atmospheric conditions back to the very perceptual basics—seeing and looking, but as well feeling and touching. We are immersing in video atmospheres.

»The new aesthetics is first of all what its name states, namely a general theory of perception. The concept of perception is liberated from its reduction to information processing, provision of data or (re)cognition of a situation. Perception includes the affective impact of the observed, the *reality of images*, corporeality. Perception is basically the manner in which one is bodily present for something or someone or one's bodily state in an environment. The primary *object* of perception is atmospheres. What is first and immediately perceived is neither sensations nor shapes or objects or their constellations, as Gestalt psychology thought, but atmospheres, against whose background the analytic regard distinguishes such things as objects, forms, colours etc.

The new aesthetics is a response to the progressive aestheticization of reality. An aesthetics, which is a theory of art or of the work of art, is completely inadequate to this task. Moreover, since it is confined to a sphere separated from action and to educated elites, it hides the fact that aesthetics represents a real social power. There are aesthetic needs and an aesthetic supply. There is, of course, aesthetic pleasure but there is also aesthetic manipulation. To the aesthetics of the work of art we can now add with equal right the aesthetics of everyday life, the aesthetics of commodities and a political aesthetics. General aesthetics has the task of making this broad range of aesthetic reality transparent and articulatable.« (Boehme 1993, 11.113)

Gernot Böhme demands a critical understanding and acting in a place and a present constructed and relying on atmospheres. Aesthetics itself has the task of thinking critically and reflecting, and should not be reduced to the arts. The critical potential of an aesthetic of atmospheres legitimizes the aesthetics of the everyday. For Böhme, because we are surrounded by atmospheres and atmosphere-building techniques of the everyday, the social and the political—which might be or even are biasing, alienating, and even blinding—a critic is already tasked with showing the feasibility of atmospheres to break their suggestive powers and create playfulness toward them. By their nature, atmospheres are gripping and grasping, immersive. They are forms of realness, which appear to be real or to be reality. Video is a substantial element, a method and technology for the realization of atmosphere; in itself, it creates atmosphere.

THE EDITING ROOM PARADIGM

What shall we do with all this video?

To meaningfully analyze such an ocean of material might only be methodologically possible if we construct a deductive or inductive conclusion by zooming in and out, moving and scanning freely through the present phenomenon that we call video—or, more broadly speaking, digital moving images or time-based changing images or image parts.

As guidance and examples of such a methodology, this text will relate to the practice and process of postproduction of audiovisual objects, sequences, and events. In its concrete manifestation, it means adopting methods and practices of the film editing room as a model with which to investigate online video.

Thinking in an editing room paradigm means, first of all, thinking in a simple, very traditional and historical way about a huge amount of material that will be handled, logged, evaluated, sorted, and prepared in meaningful chunks. It is a subjective process. It is, of course, analog.

The material—video—is split into smaller parts, units, or elements, which we can call "clips." The split material in the editing room is logged and annotated; metadata is added; it is time-stamped, indexed, sorted into bins related to various kinds of principles, affects, keywords, mechanics, and so on. The bins later are split again into trim bins, the clips in subclips to build sequences; the editor conceives of items or objects as keyframes, timelines, heads, or heads and tails, forming linear strings and flows of events, creating beginnings and endings, rearranging, fine-tuning, vertical adjusting with layered shapes, graphics, sounds; the color is graded and processed for a single version while keeping the original clip untouched.

This text proposes a rethinking of the conceptualization of digital nonlinear moving image editing; it involves conceptualizing a new workflow of software for such an editing practice to organize meaningful singular cases of online video and relate them to an overall formal aesthetic principle of shaping a cultural object—even shaping culture itself through its essentially atmospheric material video.

The digital video revolution of the early 2000s already addressed the problem of exponential increase of material in the editing or assemblage stage, calling for a modification of traditional editing and audiovisual postproduction methods, a multiplication of the process. A single editor was no longer able to handle all the material, to know all the shots to be considered. Of course, one of the main reasons for the increase in material was the enormous decrease of production costs, making recording equipment and materials available for consumers and gaining comparable high-quality results.

Video has always been assembled (RE: Assemblies of Video 2013). Such an assemblage has always been a cultural form built by other assemblages, which again were assembled by other ones. As online video, it is reassembled in new contexts, levels, affordances, customizations and personalizations. Thinking about editing means engaging with a *structural* analysis of online video culture. This is a process-oriented viewing of online video that considers that temporary items are the basic substance for construction of meanings. These temporary items could be seen as little bricks similar to video bricks. They can assemble into any kind of shape or spatial object. It is like Lego for moving images or LEGO made of moving-image-based temporary objects. The moving image or video is the plastic the brick is made of. The brick itself is a temporal category or object.

»LEGO pieces can be combined in multiple ways. But what allows them to interact effectively is the shape and structure of the bricks—the bundle of properties that allow them to snap together easily.« (Arbesman 2013)

In some way, video is a bundle of properties that allows the creation of various or multiple atmosphere-creating audiovisual temporal objects and frequencies. Video at first look appears to be solid while imitating cinematic assemblage practices, but video items might also be described as molecules, atoms, or bubbles and foam. Video items are not simply repetitive: yes, meaningful objects or units can be repeated, but rather than repetition and repeatability, it is their multifunctionality, modularity, automatism and algorithmic being that build video's multiverse of meaning. Each of the millions and millions of moving dots of light used to construct units of images and time can create in repetition something fresh and therefore new. It can be another sequence initiated from the same material, but it can also create another connection to and with another materiality, or open up another sphere or aura.

In the editing paradigm, the smallest possible element or item for video as moving image is a clip. The short-form video-sharing service Vine, for example, combines a maximum of three small clips into a six-second video. It emphasizes a practice of use of small short units, or shots, or clips. A clip must be differentiated from the "shot" of classical cinematography. Vine, and the definition of the clip, raise the question of duration. What is the impact of videos limited to a few seconds? Can we set them in the tradition of short Flash animations or animated gifs? Is the flood of online videos related to a way of seeing and viewing/showing? What is the meaning of the loop and its rebirth through applications like Vine and various practices on the web?

Clips can be created en masse and if constituted as bricks reassembled over and over, creating endless variations of cultural expressions. Technically storage is needed only for new recordings and renders, but not for new assemblages as the material is already stored somewhere on a server or multiple servers.

In a further analytical step, in the editing room the sorted and indexed clip is evaluated by its graphical quality. Independent from any metadata attached, the clip is evaluated formally and aesthetically by its shape and the shapes of its framed content. Once again here the question of framing something as a recording or as a moving image becomes relevant and all too obvious.

The advent of video-enabled smartphones violates cinematic conventions through their acceptance of verticality—it's natural to hold a smartphone vertically instead of horizontally, so the natural frame shape is taller than it is wide, unlike film formats. This links online video aesthetics very closely to mobile devices and breaks with embedded cinematic conditions. Beyonce's rehearsal video from 2011, which was shot by her husband on his mobile device, serves as an exemplary vertical video, questioning the act of framing and the authenticity of the depicted. Beyonce's video questions the shape of video and opens up to discussions of the influence of the frame as shape as well as the shape itself on the viewer and user.

In the next part of this approach, I'll discuss interiors and exteriors of video, the question of video surfaces and insides. Robert Ochshorn's approach of rethinking compression and his look inside video in projects like *Montage Interdit* will be a starting point to explore what happens when you step into a clip as a nest—an already existing assemblage—and what happens when you extend a clip through spatial layering, thickening and expanding it, building multiple relations with multiple objects of other kinds. As the code of the web comes to understand video, video can become code-like and code might become video-like. The world, our world can then be understood as process or as in process.

Finally, we look at instances of space making, atmospheres, environmental conditions, sabotages and noise making through online video.

Online video seems to overlie as a living system of noise our physical world. It's a dust slowly building layer-by-layer, thickening and changing regional climates. This noise of video can only be deciphered through various kinds of patterns in multiple layers, patterns we already know as cultural artifacts and constants. More interesting than the patterns might be the noise, as Michel Serres points out:

»Background noise is the ground of our perception, absolutely uninterrupted, it is our perennial sustenance, the element of the software of all our logic. It is the residue and the cesspool of our messages. No life without heat, no matter, neither; no warmth without air, no logos without noise, either. Noise is the basic element of the software of all our logic, or it is to the logos what matter used to be to form. Noise is the background of information, the material of that form.« (Serres 1995, 7)

At the end of the text is the beginning repeated. In looking at the space-making ability of video, we consider again the exploration of multiple possible worlds and forms of existence. In the overall processes of *view, overview, looking at,* and *looking in,* video neutralizes an overloaded single world through an experience of lights and colors not transformed by the dictatorship and domination of narrative structure and design. Video is the pure change of light in time.

VIDEO UNCHAINED

> The electronic image is a marvelous tool for dreaming. I thought I was opening up a path that all of television could take, and I am the lone hero of a lost battle.
> JEAN-CHRISTOPHE AVERTY

> There is something vertiginous in the video image, in its rationale, in its very being. How can one not see, in the myriad dots that make up its frame, a welter of ideas, drawing in those seeking to recognize themselves in the image and tending to take a lateral course, to join at least some of the dots together? By what it invites us to represent, the video image is one of the keenest manifestations of thought, of its jumps and disorderliness. Through thought as image, it gives us an image of thought, vibrant, and unstable.
> RAYMOND BELLOUR/BETWEEN THE IMAGES

VIDEO AS FORM OF LIFE

When the French director Jean-Christophe Averty wrote that video is "a marvelous tool for dreaming," of course he was referring to television and the moving image recorded in its electromagnetic form of an analog signal. As the electronic moving image has evolved, we have begun to actually daydream with digital video on the web and with our mobile devices, phones, and tablets.

If a life form is something with its own development, changing and growing, then web-driven video has become a life form. »Web video« is one of the major communication forms of Internet culture. It is no longer just a shared audiovisual, temporal object of affect and interest.

What is »web video«? Is it different from other cultural forms of the moving image like cinema, television, or video art? Is there a distinguished, genuine form? Are there genres, typologies evolving or already evolved? (MovingWeb 2011)[1]

The video we are experiencing today—in its forms, practices, and theories—is different from the video people used and experienced years ago, even a month ago. It also differs greatly from other established forms of moving image.[2]

The lifelike video and its digitally coded imaginary constantly references other images, other connected videos, objects, and things, relations to other people, things, and the world outside our bodies. It stands in relation to our bodies and their positions and variations. The time reference of a video can be multiple even it is just now when it is played. The image itself is not a flat carrier of single identifiable messages anymore; rather, it expands and gains volume through its constructed relations with things. The video image is a temporal, thickened image. This thickened image is relational to the world, things, and us existing with it in co-relation.

Of course, a philosophical idea inspired by Peter Sloterdijk's *Spheres* trilogy, literally taken, formulates and suggests an understanding of these

---

[1] Some questions asked for a survey on web video on MovingWeb: »But what distinguishes video on the World Wide Web from other media like TV, video (art) or film? Which genuine forms and genres evolve on platforms like YouTube, Vimeo & Co?«

[2] With the image of spheres as described in *The Inner Life of Video Spheres* in 2013 I had already tried to explain how we share a space with video, how video lives with us. We are moving together. We are diving even in an ocean of video (Treske 2013).

phenomena of environments, worlds, as similar to bubbles attaching to other bubbles, coming together to form foam. Society is imagined as a sphere through the technological, environment-constructing video. Video is not just a representation. Video is not just a technological relation of our bodies, our environments, our selves, and us. It is a companion.

This imaginary world of bubbles and foam as a metaphorical approach to explain complex conditions of observation sounds like the record of an observation sitting in a bubble bath and reflecting on the white creamy foam, each of the bubbles a single video forming the spherical object through its own environmental extension—a video linking to a map, a photo, a text, a Wikipedia article, and so on. The imagination as a round object helps us see all the things together, which are initiated or related by that single video. Bubbles, foam and sphere are metaphors to think about the construction of atmospheres and atmospheric relations in our world through everyday online video. They are imaginary objects expanded in hybrid space—virtual and real.

»The new aesthetics is thus as regards the producers a general theory of aesthetic work, understood as the production of atmospheres. As regards reception it is a theory of perception in the full sense of the term, in which perception is understood as the experience of the presence of persons, objects and environments.« (Boehme 1993, 116)

FOREST VIEWING

If we look at a video, do we see a video? What do we see? What do we look at? Is that still a physical scene we look at? In which context are we looking at it? Are we moving toward the video or is the video moving toward us?

In a painting by the Turkish painter Şeker Ahmet (1841–1907) a woodcutter looks into a forest. When he looks at the trees, all trees, the close ones close and those far, far away are not only huge, they are equal in their sizes.

Illustration 1: Woodcutter in the Forest, Şeker Ahmet

Source: Museum of Painting and Sculpture, Beşiktaş, Istanbul

»There is something deeply but subtly strange about the perspective, about the relationship between the woodcutter with his mule and the far edge of the forest in the top right-hand corner. You see that it is the far edge, and, at the same time, that third distant tree (a beech?) appears nearer than anything else in the painting. It simultaneously withdraws and approaches.« (Berger 1991, 87)

The woodcutter does not see the forest. His perspective is reversed. He is part of the forest. Therefore his experience of the forest differs from that of another observer. This distant observer would have placed a scene inside the forest, as John Berger pointed out. The distant observer would have seen the scene rather than the trees themselves. A hierarchical setting would have been created. The woodcutter in the painting would be emphasized in the order through color, light, or size. His size would be in a hierarchical relation built through Renaissance perspective to other objects depicted in the forest.

The painting marks a »disjuncture« and there receives its importance. Şeker Ahmet was educated in Paris and knew very well to paint a forest in the Western tradition, but he saw something else. What he saw and painted depicts a different relationship to the world around. It is not a world adapted, conquered, modified, it's a world having its own presence. The forest is a thing »taking place in itself.... You make your way through the forest and, simultaneously, you see yourself, as from the outside, swallowed by the forest. What gives this painting its peculiar authority is its faithfulness to the experience of the figure of the woodcutter« (Berger 1991, 88, 91).

Unlike European painting, the Turkish or Ottoman tradition was based on miniatures, small illustrations in books, many rooted in Persian traditions. These illustrations depicted a spiritual space and were very closely related to the way stories were told.

»The novel, as Lukacs pointed out in *Theory of the Novel*, was born of a yearning for what now lay beyond the horizon: it was the art-form of a sense of homelessness. With this homelessness came an openness of choice (most novels are primarily about choices) such as man had never experienced before. Earlier narrative forms are more two-dimensional, but not for that reason less real. Instead of choice, there is pressing necessity. Each event is unavoidable as soon as it is present. The only choices are about treating, coming to terms with, what is there. One can talk about immediacy, but since all events narrated in this way are immediate, the term changes its meaning. Events come into being like the genie of Aladdin's lamp. They are equally irrefutable, expected and unexpected.« (Berger 1991, 90)

The forest in Seker Ahmet's painting is coming into being. John Berger links the painting to the German philosopher Martin Heidegger's use of the forest as a symbol of reality in his »Conversation on a Country Path about Thinking.«

»The task of philosophy is to find the *Weg*, the woodcutter's path, through the forest. The path may lead to the *Lichtung*, the clearing whose very space, open to light and vision, is the most surprising thing about existence, and is the very condition of Being. 'The clearing is the opening for everything that is present and absent.'« (Berger 1991, 92)

Şeker Ahmet's painting reflects the »coming-into-the-nearness of distance« as thinking. The woodcutter in the painting approaches the forest, but the forest, the distant, also approaches the woodcutter.

»For Heidegger the present, the now, is not a measurable unit of time, but the result of presence, of the existent actively presenting itself. In his attempt to bend language

to describe this, he turns the word presence into a verb: presencing. Tentatively, Novalis prefigured this when he wrote: 'Perceptibility is a kind of attentiveness.'
The woodcutter and his mule are stepping forward. Yet the painting renders them almost static. They are scarcely moving. What is moving—and this is so surprising that one senses it without at first being able to realize it—is the forest. The forest with its presence is moving in the opposite direction to the woodcutter—i.e., forward towards us and leftwards. 'Presence means: the constant abiding that approaches man, reaches him, is extended to him.« (Berger 1991, 93)

MY NAME IS RED

The novel *My Name Is Red* by Turkish Nobel Prize winner Orhan Pamuk is another elaboration of an *Eastern* concept of art. Painting is referred to as an act of memory. The murder story of the novel builds on the secret commission of a great book by the Sultan in 1590. The book should be a celebration of his life and his empire. The sultan wants it to be illustrated by the best artists in a European style. This, of course, is a heresy as it breaks with the classic style and Islamic tradition.

Classic miniatures can be characterized as depicting figures impersonally. The miniatures stand strictly as illustrations of the text, which they accompany. The Sultan in the novel asks for paintings in the style of the Italian Renaissance. He wants individual figures. He wants his specific portrait. These are paintings that stand on their own as works of art. The conflict of perspective is the creation of things as they appear to the naked eye.

»'Every picture serves to tell a story,' I said. The miniaturist, in order to beautify the manuscript we read, depicts the most vital scenes: the first time lovers lay eyes on each other; the hero Rüstem cutting off the head of a devilish monster; Rüstem's grief when he realizes that the stranger he's killed is his son; the love-crazed Mejnun as he roams a desolate and wild Nature among lions, tigers, stags and jackals; the anguish of Alexander, who, having come to the forest before a battle to divine its outcome from the birds, witnesses a great falcon tear apart his woodcock. Our eyes, fatigued from reading these tales, rest upon the pictures. If there's something within the text that our intellect and imagination are at pains to conjure, the illustration comes at once to our aid. The images are the story's blossoming in color. But painting without its accompanying story is an impossibility.« (Pamuk 1998/2001, 30)

And as in opposition, Pamuk describes the description and the reaction of the master of a painting seen in a palace in Venice:

»More than anything, the image was of an individual, somebody like myself. It was an infidel, of course, not one of us. As I stared at him, though, I felt as if I resembled him. Yet he didn't resemble me at all. He had a full round face that seemed to lack cheekbones, and moreover, he had no trace of my marvelous chin. Though he didn't look anything like me, as I gazed upon the picture, for some reason, my heart fluttered as if it were my own portrait....

The Venetian virtuoso had made the nobleman's picture in such a way that you would immediately know which particular nobleman it was. If you'd never seen that man, if they told you to pick him out of a crowd of a thousand others, you'd be able to select the correct man with the help of that portrait. The Venetian masters had discovered painting techniques with which they could distinguish any one man from another—without relying on his outfit or medals, just by the distinctive shape of his face. This was the essence of 'portraiture.'

If your face were depicted in this fashion only once, no one would ever be able to forget you, and if you were far away, someone who laid eyes on your portrait would feel your presence as if you were actually nearby. Those who had never seen you alive, even years after your death, could come face-to-face with you as if you were standing before them.« (Pamuk 1998/2001, 31)

Video has always been thought of as realistic or even over-realistic. It depicts the world as it is seen. In the context of the web and its digital evolution, I propose that video has left this realm and is linked to a different way of world-constructing. Video came closer to concepts of Eastern understanding of world and society. What video has become, like Şeker Ahmet's forest, looks back at us.

Master Osman in Pamuk's novel describes a classic miniature of a legend of two lovers, which sums up somehow this idea and the connection to Seker Ahmet's painting in a beautiful Rilkean way:

»It's as if the lovers are to remain here eternally within the light emanating from the painting's texture, skin and subtle colors which were applied lovingly by the miniaturist. You can see how their faces are turned ever so slightly toward one another while their bodies are half-turned toward us—for they know they're in a painting and thus visible to us. This is why they don't try to resemble exactly those figures, which we see around us. Quite to the contrary, they signify that they've emerged from Allah's memory.« (Pamuk 1998/2001, 411)

PERSON OF INTEREST

While rethinking the question of seeing—what do we see and how do we see?—we become aware not only *that* we are seeing but also that we are looked at. The videos we are producing are producing us as well. It seems paradoxical. If video is everywhere, and video is attached to any kind of device, object, thing, and this is networked, then obviously there is surveillance. This is a seeing different than our own. We are not only watched by what was somehow an ideological construct of the Big Brother idea, suggesting that there is somewhere someone watching. We are simply looked at by anything we are in relation with, or touched by, or touching. We are followed live and in real time. Our sense of curiosity, our concern with things surrounding us, brings up automatically a concern of things with us. Our "interest" stimulates our senses, our arousing, and our excitement of an opportunity of involvement with anything.

In the 2011 television series *Person of Interest*, a U.S. government computer system called the Machine is programmed to monitor and analyze data from surveillance cameras and electronic communications. The purpose is to foresee terrorist attacks and predict violent activities. Instead of just detecting terrorism, the Machine was also programmed to access non-relevant data and detect all kinds of future violent acts. The finding of social security numbers among the non-relevant data motivates each episode and storyline (Nolan 2011).

The TV series tries to give its audience a subjective view of the world as the Machine sees it through adding on, overlaying, and filling the screen of the show (or its frame) with multiple frames of images and footage from surveillance cameras, zooming back and moving over layers and layers of video footage around the globe, turning back or zooming in on a single location with tracked moving objects and persons in it referenced by small attached frames and numbers.

The Machine sees and is looking at the world while constantly tracking and analyzing movement data. Each Machine-generated on-screen display shows the audience data about a character or characters: identification, their activities, and their records. The location is suggested to be the world, but is mainly New York. Green triangles outline commercial flights over the city, red concentric circles indicate no-fly zones, and dashed boxes mark individual people. Color-coding classifies the people. Red, of course, is used for people the Machine perceives as threats.

The Machine communicates with the main characters through telephones and social security numbers to help them assist people under threat.

»You are being watched. The government has a secret system: a machine that spies on you every hour of every day. I know, because I built it. I designed the machine to detect acts of terror, but it sees everything. Violent crimes involving ordinary people; people like you. Crimes the government considered 'irrelevant'. They wouldn't act, so I decided I would. But I needed a partner, someone with the skills to intervene. Hunted by the authorities, we work in secret. You'll never find us, but victim or perpetrator, if your number's up... we'll find you.« (Nolan 2011)

While we as observers are surveying roads, traffic, airports, hotel lobbies, and so on, the surveillance technology we are using looks back at us and registers any movement of the observers.

Surveillance as a theme in cinema or television is not new. A remarkable film based on surveillance footage is Chris Marker's short flash movie *Stopover in Dubai*. Marker uses video surveillance footage released by the Dubai police to document the killing of the Hamas operative Mahmoud al Mabhouh by the Israeli secret service.

»Whether the fascination of this derives from the dense interplay of some 14 or perhaps 26 players, some changing costumes and disguises, delivering messages, or from the furtive glances of the victim as he goes to his room where death awaits him, I am not sure. Or perhaps it is from the frisson of knowing before the fact that one is observing the preparations for an actual murder. Or perhaps it is from the sequence of unstated matters—the expense of all these characters being flown first to Dubai, checking into multiple classy hotels, coordinating via calls to an Austrian telephone exchange, leaving after the job was done apparently without checking out from the hotel, or leaving a long trail of evidence as shown in these images. The real 'action' of the film is all off-screen—the entry into the victim's room, the room opposite visited by a long string of accomplices, the actual killing. One wonders why the hallway is not shown—surely there must be a surveillance camera that observed it. Or such mysteries as how did they gain access to the room, and then how did they leave the room such that the internal latch was set to lock? And why did Mossad hire a fistful of Irish, English, German, Australian and other non-Israelis to carry out this execution? ...« (Cinemaelectronica 2010).

Marker had appropriated GNTV/Dubai State Media's footage without changing it. By replacing the soundtrack with a string composition by Henryk Górecki for the Kronos Quartet he not only created a remix, but also made an entirely new film (Allen 2012). He did not manipulate the image, but did manipulate the sound, shifting or switching from an ambient sound to a structured, emotional composition. The assembled footage and the recording of the Kronos Quartet change the emotional perception and status of the seen.

TV VIEWING

Looking back at the viewer entered another technological level in September 2013 as news spread that LG smart television sets actually track their users and their program choices live, and send this information back to the company's headquarters.

Television producers like LG, Samsung, and Sony are able to use the built-in technologies in their connected smart televisions to tell what audiences are watching. This information is of great interest and value for marketers as well as TV producers. The collected data can determine program ratings and audience behaviors. The manufacturers not only opened up new advertising venues but also raised privacy concerns.

It is becoming obvious that any smart technology will always work in multiple ways. This includes phones, computers, tablets, and television sets as well as cars, watches, or any personal technological items. Any manufacturer or provider will work with the resulting and more or less automatically available data.

Television is viewing us.

A MACHINE TO SEE WITH

»Just listen to the voice on the phone. The voice tells you what to do. The voice says you're playing the lead in a movie. Hide in the toilets, find the getaway car, stake out the bank and take a deep breath. You're going in.« (Blast Theory 2012)

A Machine to See With is a locative cinema game by the British artist group Blast Theory. It was commissioned by the Sundance Film Festival, the 01 San Jose Biennial and the Banff New Media Institute and premiered in September 2010 in San Jose. Participants give their mobile numbers when they sign up to play the lead in a film. When the game starts, the participant receives an automated call giving a location to go to. A series of telephoned instructions to change locations follows. The participant becomes a character in a heist movie where a bank robbery takes place. Although the story is fiction, it is set in a real city and a real bank.

The work by Blast Theory builds on basic ideas related to cinema. The city is understood as a cinematic space and the eyes of the participants as the screens themselves. Blast Theory cite Chris Hedges on their website to *A Machine to See With*:

»We try to see ourselves moving through our life as a camera would see us, mindful of how we hold ourselves, how we dress, what we say. We invent movies that play in our heads.« (Blast Theory 2012)

Blast Theory's starting point »was *Made in USA* by Jean-Luc Godard and the novel from which he *stole* the story, *The Jugger* by Richard Stark.«

»The book is a classic of arid compressed noir. Godard took the story as a springboard for a commentary on the Vietnam War, mixing trashy violence with contemporary politics. The title of the work is taken from Godard's script for *Pierrot Le Fou* in which Jean Paul Belmondo's character says, 'my eyes are a machine to see with'.« (Blast Theory 2012)

It is about the tyranny of choice and consumerism. The work uses an open-source piece of call center software called *Asterisk* and thus employs automation to create an ostensibly personalized experience. Adam Curtis' film *Eight People Sipping Wine in Kettering* explores the rise of focus groups and marketing based on desire rather than need. Aspects of these polling questions crop up in the work during a section that presumes to create a psychological profile of each participant. Robert Reich's book *Locked in the Cabinet* explores one aspect of this process in detail, looking at the 1996 US presidential election when Bill Clinton attempted to get reelected against the odds and set up a large call center in Denver to poll thousands of swing voters every day. Some participants hear this story as they wait in the getaway car.

»It is about the financial crisis. With the attempted robbery of a bank at its heart, money is a recurrent part of the work. It contrasts the agency of a film star, of a protagonist in a heist movie with the reality of the financial crisis since 2008. It places the adrenaline rush of revenge against the steady impotence of citizens confronted by global capitalism.« (Blast Theory 2012)

Blast Theory take mixed-reality gaming as a social activity, as a performative event, and as a spectacle. The work is an exploration of interactivity and the relationship between real and virtual space (mixed reality) with a particular focus on the social and political aspects of technology and in this specific case with a link to and mash-up of cinema.

Blast Theory's works require access to mobile communication and networks to mediate their work. Their special interest focuses on devices, handset, headset, PDAs and networks to be used for messaging and transferring data of locations and actions via text, video, and audio. Their activity establishes a cultural space in the city. They add the virtual layer of a cinematic space with a dramatic action narrative taking place.

»This is not a personality test. This is A Machine To See With. The ending is up to you. In 8 seconds I will hang up. You will not hear from me again. Goodbye.« (Blast Theory 2012)

CITIZEN WORM

At the first annual Phone Film Festival, organized in 2013 by Easter Mediterranean University in North Cyprus, *Citizen Worm*, directed by Iranian graduate student Arman Arian, won the Best Short Film prize. Arian's film serves as an example how our observation of the world we are living in is already cinematic (Arian 2013). Shot with a mobile phone like all of the submissions, the film opens with a subjective view between grasses and bushes; sounds of movement fill the soundtrack. A parallel edit introduces a person bicycling. The cutting sequence now goes in a nearly classic cinematic style with the melody of a guitar from trees, to the bicycle wheel, to the cyclist's shadow on the road. Then there's a cut to a subjective view similar to the opening shot, this time showing the road in very close detail. Something moves forward: this close subjective shot tells us that it is very small. The mobile phone camera tilts slightly upward and we see the opposite side of a road, which the thing wants to cross or will cross. The director repeats the shaky tilt movement several times, intensifying the need to cross the road; showing the tires of a car passing in one of the tilts introduces danger. Again cut to the wheel of the bicycle, cut to the other side of the wheel, showing the same wheel turning, cut to another shot of the bicycle and a sudden accidental movement and fade to black. After the fade, a title gives place, date, and time on black, then another fade opens up the image to a much more documentary type of observation of caterpillar larvae in a long row coming out of the greens and starting to cross the street.

The five-minute film narrates their story of crossing a street continuously driven over by cars. Only a few larvae are able to survive and cross. At the end, the filmmaker delivers as a text on a blurred image the statement that from one thousand immigrants only a small group and one single survived crossing a three-meter asphalt desert.

The nonprofessional short film clearly develops a narrative and builds a narrative structure. Its filmmaker possesses cinematic literacy and expresses it in the arrangement and framing of shots, the camera positions, and of course the editing, the sequencing, and the design of structure and atmosphere. What is produced on a mobile phone appears as a film or a movie from the very first shot. The way the filmmaker sees the event of the street-crossing larvae is already structured and influenced by a cinematic language with a grammar and set of rules. What makes the process different from that of the professional is the tool (the mobile phone camera) and perhaps the sometimes imperfect control of image, light, focus and framing, which are left to the user's or filmmaker's tool, which in March 2013 was a smartphone with video-recording capabilities.

The process of seeing is structured. When we are recording video, we operate in shots and sequences, because that's what our cultural perception of cinema and television tells us to do. This might differ from person to person. It might also suggest some perfectionism—smooth, *invisible* editing—or amateurism—jumping and edging nervously.

We see our world through video, and video looks back at us. The way we see seems to be formally structured and even conditioned through a form of language. The little film by the Iranian student in a mobile film festival in North Cyprus observing an event on the street—not just documenting and following, but turning it into a dramatic, perhaps autobiographical migration story—is a way of looking, viewing and projecting a world, edited and styled as a cinematic experience with its way of shooting, changing camera positions, and narrative construction of beginning, middle, and end. Rather than specific properties of a *video seeing*, the short film recalls and projects the experience of cinema.

Video itself as a practice of seeing, a practice of looking, viewing, showing and telling, a method, procedure, process or rule in particular to the moving image is not rehearsed. The mobile phone camera rehearses and engages in a cinematic activity. The filmmaker practices her or his instrument, trains and acquires experience in cinematic production, makes herself or himself fit for the techno-social conditions we are living in.

The process of projection is one of becoming aware of the presence of video, of the world, and of oneself. Producing video as a way of looking would provide our own meanings to the world we are attempting to organize around us. Somehow we are reminded of Oedipa in Thomas Pynchon's *The Crying of Lot 49* when she writes in her notebook, »Shall I project a world?« (Pynchon 1966, 82)

SHALL I PROJECT A WORLD?

The story of Lot 49 is an investigation into the legacy of a dead father figure. It's founded on an analogy between the »projected world« of the quester's paranoia and the actual world represented by the father figure. The world is rebuilt as a fiction using projection as method (Bloom 2003, 217).

Video is set in close relation with cinema and television. Cinema and television are the objects to study, as they are already categorized, identifiable, and definable. Video itself disappears. Video, as Tom Sherman described it some years ago, is liquid and shimmering. It is an »ubiquitous medium that absorbs everything it touches« (Sherman 2008). Video itself, so it seems, has »no single or essential form« (Neves 2013). Because it is such a commonplace thing, there is no theory of video. Video even seems to resist theory. Mobile videos or short films like *Citizen Worm* always set themselves in relation to their ancestors, cinema and television. There has already been a video-specific way of making or a »videofication« in the works of avant-garde filmmakers, artists, VJs, and video activists, one that is well covered in secondary literature on video art. In the analog world, artists have explored the materiality of the electronic moving image, the audiovisual signal and its potentials—potentials that are now available to everyone, any time, anywhere.

The critic Jonathan Rosenbaum, while discussing *Soft and Hard* (1985) from Godard and Mieville in his 1995 article »Godard in the Age of Video,« refers to specific properties of video that disrupt our sense of a natural flow.

»What differentiates film from TV and video may sound like a tired subject—after all, Marshall McLuhan was already calling TV a cool medium and film a hot one back in 1964. But it's uncertain whether we understand these complex differences as well as we pretend to. Even our everyday conversations—when we talk about 'seeing a movie on video' or 'seeing a movie on television'—imply that we're seeing the same movie we'd see in a theater and not a radically transmogrified version.« (Rosenbaum 1995)

Seeing a movie today could be as well on a mobile device. The viewing is no longer bound to a fixed location. In this sense, movies left the theaters and the living rooms to enter our most intimate spaces. As objects, they walked toward us.

In 1995, Rosenbaum was still impressed by the materiality of the video viewing. He sympathizes with Godard's concerns and his struggle with an image of an obviously different presence and materiality than the film or photographic image ever had. Rosenbaum formulates Godard synthesizes his concerns of the prosaic, anti-metaphoric, and *objective* side of television in a climactic meditation in *Soft and Hard* on film and video:

»Cinema projects itself in a form of visual representation that people can recognize, so that the 'I' could be projected, enlarged, and could get lost. But its idea could still be traced back; there was a sort of metaphor. Television, on the other hand, can project nothing but us. So you no longer know where the subject is. In cinema, in the very idea of the large screen, like the myth of Plato's cave, [you get] the idea of project, projection (which, in French at least, have the same roots: 'project,' 'projection,' 'subject'). With TV, on the other hand, you feel you take it in—you're subjugated by it, so to speak. You become its subject, like the subject of a king.« (Rosenbaum 1995)

Even more than television, the digital video on the web closes in on the subject as it surrounds it. A generation born in cinema will ask for a distant photographic image, moved or transported. Growing up with television then prompts a need for feelings against an objectified image. This image needs to be overcome. Today, this image is already replaced, as it became another fiction created through software.

Like in Godard's *Soft and Hard,* the playful use of freeze-frames, slurred motion, and superimpositions are obvious statements in producing difference. They explore potentials embedded in an analog view. It is the exploration of a materiality that belongs to a past for which only nostalgia or *retro* design, citation, and quoting show technological appreciation. This is significant in the archeology of media; it helps to set continuity. A linear technological narrative is produced, smoothing the transition between the analog and the digital. This technological narrative does not directly suggest a paradigm change.

Similar to *cinephilia*, where you have celluloid films as objects of appreciation and collection, looking back to analog video and television creates nostalgia for a materiality and physicality the digital seems to lack. The touch of the digital is not even *cold*.

Does it still make sense to consider McLuhan's distinction of *hot and cold* media? A *hot* movie is filled with information; it has a high density. Photography has it too, whereas cartoons lack density or are of low definition. Radio is of high definition, whereas the telephone is of low. But television requires a great deal of participation, whereas cinemas require little.

The user of a telephone, much like the television viewer, must supplement the low level of information by maximizing participation. Video on the web is embedded, not only in websites and software interfaces, but in our environment. We are already an active element of the completeness—it's not just our active participation, it is we, together with the video that completes. Low information again means maximum participation.

With cinema and television, or radio and photography, it is relatively easy to relate to objects of study. There are distinct and clear artifacts. Online video is not that easy to see as a single object to be categorized and understand. Yes, video is a mass-produced temporal object viewed and listened to by millions simultaneously (Stiegler 2010, 1). Temporal industrial objects are the determining elements of the present. Video in its short technological history has always been seen as deriving from television. Video art, as Raymond Bellour summarized in 1986, »is inextricably intertwined with television.« And it »sees its mirror image in television« (Bellour 2012). Online video went beyond this view. What programming industries used as a technical vehicle is now embedded in a web of social relations in a social space. Video has no single object that can be separated. Video itself—once defined as a clear object such as the videocassette—is immersed in layers of interactive assemblages, much like the web itself.

»We make the case that there are more continuities than often recognized between analogue and digital; that transitional forms like video have not been analyzed sufficiently; that software studies needs to be backed up with hardware studies; and that there is a new role for medium-specific criticism. We argue that, in the current state of digital resources for production, distribution and display, each work needs to be analyzed in its specificity, rather than ascribing universal qualities to imaginary abstractions such as 'digital media'.« (Cubitt et al. 2011, 37)

FLOODED

»YouTube is full of videos, millions of them. Entertaining videos. Informative videos. Instructional videos. You name it, somebody has probably uploaded a video about it.« (Miller 2010, 1)

Video is everywhere …

This sounds disastrous. It is a flood. Video on the web is exponentially growing. The amount of video uploaded on the web increases by millions of gigabytes daily. Not an ocean, not a weather change with slow-rising rivers leaving their beds—no, a tsunami ...

The most prominent video-sharing website, biggest video jukebox, or one of the big leaks is YouTube. The site was created in February 2005 and bought by Google in 2006. Since then it has become the front outlet, and public symbol for online video sharing.

YouTube, as Jean Burgess writes, is the »first mass-popular platform for user-created media content. It launched without knowing exactly what it was for, and it is this under-determination that explains the scale and diversity of its uses today« (Burgess 2009).

The content of YouTube is co-created by the corporate, professional, everyday, and organizational users who upload videos to the website, and an audience or audiences who engage with the videos. It still fails to clearly identify its purpose and aims; it appears to be a collaboratively shaped social network and a popular open archive, which of course conflicts with Google's commercial interests.

In January 2014, YouTube reported that between 2013 and 2014, the number of uploads nearly doubled, and now »100 hours of video are uploaded to YouTube every minute« (YouTube 2014).

Already in 2010, Cisco Systems Inc., the world's largest manufacturer of routers and switches, saw Internet traffic quadrupling by 2014 and online video as its driving force.

As Tom Sherman noted on Facebook: »Clearly we are living in an era dominated by an unprecedented abundance of video information.«

New mobile devices and electronic gadgets, increasing popularity of video sites like YouTube, and online video services like Netflix create a further drive and increase IP traffic on the web.

Most significant is the very fast development of tablet personal computers initiated with the launch of Apple's iPad in 2010. The device provides easy web access, inviting users to surf the web any time they're in transition, such as at airports or in the subway. Non-places, using Marc Auge's terminology, are surf places, providing instant access to video spaces or other virtual locations (Auge 1995). In a place of non-identity, the tablet is the ideal device to open a window into another space between the user and the software.

The success of the iPad comes not from its video abilities but from thousands of small software applications (called apps) that provide an incredible variety of tools and simple playful entertainment or consumption, including video in the form of clips and streamed programs, cannibalizing various media outlets including newspapers, television, and cinema. With iPads and *smart* tablet personal devices, a second screen moves into our homes and workspaces.

The year 2013 marked a change in people's online viewing habits: Netflix announced that the company's data »shows that the majority of streamers would actually prefer to have a whole season of a show available to watch at their own pace« (J. Jurgensen 2013).

Netflix had made every episode of its political drama series *House of Cards* available to its subscribers on February 1—something no television network had ever done. Traditionally, US television networks would launch a season with a pilot and episode and watch the ratings.

At the 2013 Edinburgh International Television Festival, lead actor Kevin Spacey talked about the success of the series:

»The audience wants the control. They want the freedom. If they want to binge [...] let them binge. [...] Through this new form of distribution we have demonstrated that we have learned the lesson, the music industry didn't learn: Give people what they want, when they want it, in the form they want it in, at a reasonable price and they'll more likely pay for it rather than steal it.« (Röscheisen n.d.)

Binge viewing and in-transition viewing are becoming social norms. Viewing habits are evolving toward models of streaming ultra-short forms like Vine videos and ultra-long forms like a full season of a TV series at once. This means an ultra-expanded range of temporal audiovisual objects or moving images for viewing between extremes—full immersion in a fictional world or attention deficit in transitional settings.

Binge viewing is not just an American phenomena resulting from the easy availability of network connections and streaming media services. The success of Turkish television series in the Middle East, the Balkans, Eastern

Europe, and the former Russian republics shows a tendency to ultra-long narratives and spending entire evenings on one show; these viewings are achieved through commercial digital television and satellite television.

THE IMPOSSIBILITY OF VIEWING

It is clear that it is impossible to watch all the videos produced or available right now.

Cinema and television are built on the concept of singular objects, which means that a film—a temporal cinematic or audiovisual object—would be accessible and viewed once. In the context of television, the object is programmed as an event at a specific time and place or has to be purchased as a physical object (a DVD) or through a time-independent streaming service. Cinema and television, as programmed events, require the reservation of a specific time and schedule for viewing. Television had already eased this condition by bringing the filmic object into the home, but it still needs a programmed screening and scheduling of time slots. Both cinema and television condition a structured life. This life leaves everyday specific open slots as leisure times, which can then be filled by temporal industrial objects to be consumed. There is a time for work, and there is a time for *Freizeit* (free time).

With the Internet, the single object film is no longer available only once. Around it are multiple multiplicities of similarities, copies, extracts, variables available at the same time, the same moment and even in the same place of access, whenever. But what does this create? What kind of an audience is generated through this cultural practice and cultural technology?

The past of limited availability is over. You can find any kind of movie or film you want to watch on the web. As film scholar Dina Iordonova said in 2013, sooner or later every film ever produced or physically archived will be shared on the web (Iordonova 2013). It is just a matter of time.

So, if anything is on the network, and it's available anywhere and at any time, and there are also multiple copies, variations, appreciations, remixes, and mash-ups, what do people really watch? Netflix's research shows one phenomenon—binge-watching a single program, leaving the remote control of the 1980s on the table. Other research by the Pew Research Center from 2013 shows that »80% of adults watch online video, posting 30%, comedy, educational and how to videos top the list, ...« (Pew Research Center 2013).

With all these videos uploaded, shared, mixed, and reloaded, how do you find a single video? How much time does it take to figure out how to access and navigate this enormous and lively web archive of video? How do we find orientation, or who is orienting us?

Why do certain videos or moving images reach us, while others remain forgotten or will never reach us? Why do only certain events seem to matter?

How can we find meaning in this endless stream of video content? What kinds of methodologies are helpful to describe, analyze, and evaluate web video—methodologies for us as single users or viewers, but also methodologies for a general making of meaning? What needs to be developed to foster a deeper understanding of the underlying processes and modes of creation, viewing and sharing, or simply of being with online video?

We don't watch this or that video on YouTube. We browse YouTube itself. YouTube is a jukebox of emotions, feelings, and algorithmic relations as each video suggests others aside and in itself. We also don't make home movies on our cell phones. We just simply record life itself. In this sense, online videos are a life in progress as well as a spatial expression of this life in progress. Video creates a sphere, which clearly redefines our relationship to our world. Space in this sphere mirrors the subjectivity of the user and determines the user's interaction with society. Online video defines a sphere of relations. The multiplicity and simultaneity of these spheres creates foams, environments of existence. Walking, moving, or scrolling through these foams employs subjective tactics and user strategies similar to navigation in game space.

Online video in its historical development as video became ubiquitous. It is as itself not anymore a *thing*. It can't be treated as *representation*. It has to be considered as a temporal network of images, sounds, things, subjects, and objects. Video spreads meaningful acts around the network, inhabited spaces, and environments.

As a ubiquitous something, online video absorbs every other medium. It is what drives the web in 2014. Whereas before video was embedded in websites as containers of presentation, now HTML5 coding becomes like video itself, meaning that the web in its basic numerical code and structure, its logic, will be video-like. Therefore, video absorbs the web.

»Video was a transformative technology which collapsed barriers erected by broadcast corporations and the art-world machine« (Miller Hocking 2013).
Artistic video practices, which evolved in the 1960s and 1970s, were a reaction to the one-way delivery system of television and its political and commercial agenda. They are also a reaction against restrictive definitions of the arts and the artist. Video in an alternative and noncommercial practice was born out of the desire to talk back to the existing system and its controlling mechanisms. It »opted to disrupt the functions of broadcast and conventional TV tools in order to radicalize imagery« (Miller Hocking 2013).

The question »What is video?« is irrelevant today. Technically, it has been described and its technological developments appear transparent. Artistically, it has become a preferred and widespread mode of artistic expression, and a commodity of the white cube.

What is becoming relevant is that online video is touching, or even merging with, object spaces in various forms and practices. In this process, online video affects these objects, their spaces, and their environments. Layers of video are clustering the view. The object exists as a skeleton. Its surface is video-like and video wrapped. Online video has become an environment itself, a space-medium.

Our present digital culture challenges the understanding of video established through screen culture and media theories. Contemporary practices on the web force a rethinking of theoretical approaches and objects toward media and beyond. The very concept of the moving image has to be rethought.

Rather than just asking the classical ontological question »what is video?« it might be worth it to concentrate on the question of »how« do we use video, how do we engage with online video?

This approach might help to develop methods to analyze and describe the observed complex structures, conditions, and contexts of this environment and culture. The question is simple: how can we orient us and map a never-ending multiplicity of simultaneous flows of web video so we can draw meaningful conclusions? How can adequate methods describe these complex environmental conditions, structures, and contexts? How should we operate with an incredible amount of diverse, multiplying videos, in which the traditional forms, the known and classified industrial temporal objects are only variations of possible media aesthetics and rhetoric?

»Studying a dynamic cultural system like YouTube requires an approach that balances the range of participants and co-created media space. Determinations about what counts as content are difficult to make from the data alone, and require an examination of the videos. At scale, this poses a challenge to the methods of cultural and media studies. The methods of media and cultural studies are particularly adept at the close, richly contextualized analysis of the local and the specific, bringing this close analysis into dialogue with context, guided by and speaking back to cultural theory. But scale at the level which YouTube represents tests the limits of the explanatory power of even the best grounded or particularist accounts—among the millions of videos hosted at YouTube, it is relatively simple to find sufficient examples of whatever phenomenon the researcher wishes to investigate; it is much more difficult to use this approach to account for how YouTube itself works as a cultural system.« (Green 2009)

TASTES & MAKERS

The question of how do we find a video might easily be answered by the circumstances under which videos find us. At one time, somebody uploads, posts, or shares a single video somewhere on a platform. The video is seen and shared again. Suddenly the video appears everywhere on different outlets. It has become popular.

Viral videos have been around for a long time. They existed long before YouTube and were shared through email starting in the mid 1990s. One recent viral video is »Gangnam Style« by the Korean singer PSY, which has more than 2 billion views as of early 2015. As YouTube has become a major tool for promoting bands and music, YouTube video plays are significant for marketers. From a marketing point of view, the number of plays, whether it was fully played, and what is happening around that specific video—commentary or playlist suggestions—are worth money.

Like lots of other companies around the world, YouTube tracks viral videos, perhaps to figure out how and why some videos go viral. In his 2011 TED talk »Why Videos Go Viral«, Kevin Allocca emphasizes the role of »tastemakers«, participative communities, and unexpectedness as characteristics of media and culture today (Allocca 2011). Everyone on the net is sharing or recreating, doing something new with something that already exists. We have gained ownership of our own popular culture. That's what defines future entertainment for Allocca.

Chris Anderson, organizer of TED talks, spoke in 2010 about web video and »crowed accelerated innovation« through web video, and the start of the global TED wave as an initiative of learning from each other through shared video:

»We're a social species. We spark off each other. It's also not news to say that the Internet has accelerated innovation. For the past 15 years, powerful communities have been connecting online, sparking off each other. If you take programmers, you know, the whole open-source movement is a fantastic instance of crowd-accelerated innovation. But what's key here is, the reason these groups have been able to connect is because their work output is of the type that can be easily shared digitally—a picture, a music file, software. And that's why what I'm excited about, and what I think is under-reported, is the significance of the rise of online video.« (Anderson 2010)

He thinks online video will rise in popularity and success because video can pack huge amounts of data, which we process. Our skills evolution is video-driven.

»Reading and writing are actually relatively recent inventions. Face-to-face communication has been fine-tuned by millions of years of evolution. That's what's made it into this mysterious, powerful thing it is. Someone speaks, there's resonance in all these receiving brains, the whole group acts together. I mean, this is the connective tissue of the human superorganism in action. It's probably driven our culture for millennia. 500 years ago, it ran into a competitor with a lethal advantage. It's right here. Print scaled. The world's ambitious innovators and influencers now could get their ideas to spread far and wide, and so the art of the spoken word pretty much withered on the vine. But now, in the blink of an eye, the game has changed again. It's not too much to say that what Gutenberg did for writing, online video can now do for face-to-face communication. So, that primal medium, which your brain is exquisitely wired for ... that just went global.« (Anderson 2010)

TRENDS & ALGORITHMS

YouTube itself tries to help to find videos for us. Its Trends Map highlights the most popular videos in major markets and regions, albeit only in the US (YouTube n.d.).

One of the trends YouTube tracked in summer 2013 was the popularity of American superheroes. Based on selective keyword searches and views of videos, Batman was the most popular superhero on YouTube, with more than 3 billion views of 71,000 hours of video (YouTube 2013). The top 10 superheroes together accounted for 10 billion views and 234,000 hours of video.

Trends are generated by algorithms that attempt to identify topics, most popular keywords, and most viewed videos. Trend maps and lists are designed not only to discover these trends but also to direct more traffic toward certain videos, reinforcing the trends. Algorithms seem to have become mystical, powerful control elements, which sort, regulate, and shape what we find, see, and even what we were looking for on the web. For the majority of people using the Internet, it is unclear exactly what algorithms are doing.

»Algorithms have developed into somewhat of a modern myth. They 'compet[e] for our living rooms' ... 'determine how a billion plus people get where they're going' ... 'have already written symphonies as moving as those composed by Beethoven' ... 'allow self-determined action on the Internet but also contain aspects of control over this action' ... and 'free us from sorting through multitudes of irrelevant results'.... How do they do all this, and more? What exactly are algorithms 'doing,' and what are the implications? Can an algorithm 'do' anything? And who or what are 'algorithms' anyway?« (Barocas et al. 2013)

Algorithms are beyond our view. It not only seems that we don't understand them, we also cannot make any analogy to any experience of this kind of logic in our lives. For most people, they appear as black boxes or black holes. We don't have any metaphors for algorithms at hand.

»… more and more of our online public discourse is taking place on private communication platforms like Twitter. These providers offer complex algorithms to manage, curate, and organize these massive networks. But there is a tension between what we understand these algorithms to be, what we need them to be, and what they in fact are. We do not have a sufficient vocabulary for assessing the intervention of these algorithms.« (Gillespie 2012)

The new marketing strategy seems to be to follow last year's news on marketing and then personalize recommendations. Algorithmic recommendation is used to analyze and interpret the relations between people and things.

»Collaborative filters algorithmically re-articulate the relationship between individual and aggregate traits, suggesting the need for social scientific theories that eschew the classic break between groups and their members.« (Seaver 2012)

The basic idea is that there are many similarities among consumers. These similarities correspond with similarities in objects. An algorithm translates these in new forms and meanings, »blending preference, identity, and similarity« (Seaver 2012). Consequently, this approach is built into online infrastructures, and therefore shapes the relations between people and things.

Trends are analyzed by not just looking at the volume of activities or objects, but by how phenomena appear; this means that algorithms are programmed to look at a particular way the data appears. With Twitter, for example, »part of the evaluation includes: Is the use of the term spiking, i.e. accelerating rapidly, or is its growth more gradual? Are the users densely interconnected into a single cluster, or does the term span multiple clusters? Are the tweets unique content, or mostly re-tweets of the same post? Is this the first time the term has trended?« (Seaver 2012) This is just one of several practices to evaluate and find out what people do and what they want, instead of doing polls, surveys, street interviews, or voting mechanisms. Each of these alternatives employs a certain technique to assess an activity or opinion.

»Beyond search, we are surrounded by algorithmic tools that offer to help us navigate online platforms and social networks, based not on what we want, but on what all of their users do. When Facebook, YouTube, or Digg offer to mathematically and in real time report what is "most popular" or "liked" or "most viewed" or "best selling" or "most commented" or "highest rated," they are curating a list whose legitimacy is built on the promise that it has not been curated, that it is the product of aggregate user activity itself. When Amazon recommends a book based on matching your purchases to those of its other customers, or Demand Media commissions news based on aggregate search queries (Anderson 2011), their accuracy and relevance depend on the promise of an algorithmic calculation paired with the massive, even exhaustive, corpus of the traces we all leave.

These algorithms produce not barometric readings but hieroglyphs. At once so clear and so opaque, they beg to be read as reliable measures of the public mind, as signs of "us." But the shape of the "us" on offer is by no means transparent. Social media tools like Twitter may be adept at mapping networks of people, if only because they provide the substrate within which these networks form and interact. Even if they cannot as easily capture the human networks that extend beyond their own services, they certainly can claim to have scrutinized the part that is rendered on and by their system. However, though they aspire to with algorithmic tools like Trends, they may not be as adept at identifying or forging the publics that emerge from those networks.« (Seaver 2012)

THE JUNGLE OF SIGNS

»Hello. It is Christmas time and I am sitting here by my TV. I've been watching it very much lately because I'm on holiday. And I've been seeing all these programs about all sorts of things. About Icelandics being very happy about Christmas, very gay, and also very serious and spiritual. And also seeing Icelandic comic people making jokes. Which they are very good at.
But now I'm curious. I've switched the TV off and now I want to see how it operates. How it can make, put me into all those weird situations. So... It's about time.
This is what it looks like. Look at this. This looks like a city. Like a little model of a city. The houses, which are here, and streets. This is maybe an elevator to go up there. And here are all the wires. These wires, they really take care of all the electrons when they come through there. They take care that they are powerful enough to get all the way through to here. I read that in a Danish book. This morning.

This beautiful television has put me, like I said before, in all sorts of situations. I remember being very scared because an Icelandic poet told me that not like in cinemas, where the thing that throws the picture from it just sends light on the screen, but this is different. This is millions and millions of little screens that send light, some sort of electric light, I'm not really sure. But because there are so many of them, and in fact you are watching very many things when you are watching TV. Your head is very busy all the time to calculate and put it all together into one picture. And then because you're so busy doing that, you don't watch very carefully what the program you are watching is really about. So you become hypnotized. So all that's on TV, it just goes directly into your brain and you stop judging it's right or not. You just swallow and swallow. This is what an Icelandic poet told me. And I became so scared to television that I always got headaches when I watched it. Then, later on, when I got my Danish book on television, I stopped being afraid because I read the truth, the scientific truth and it was much better. You shouldn't let poets lie to you.« (Madrigal 2013)

The metaphor of the city for producing programs—miniature lives of miniature residents who we watch, a photomosaic of millions and millions of tiny screens—undoubtedly creates sympathy and understanding in our minds. There is a truth in describing a naive thinking that we might have experienced ourselves. There also might be a library of similar images to which unconsciously and automatically relate.

The Björk video is just one video found (perhaps) by coincidence on the web, perhaps through a search with the keywords *Björk* and *television*, leading to other videos of interviews of Björk or videos of her songs in the YouTube jukebox. Individually, the videos might appear in a different order for each of us depending on our former searches and the preferences the algorithm has set for us. Even if we did not search for Björk, a video of her might have appeared randomly on our screen.

Nevertheless, staying with the metaphoric world of Björk's description of television, the web could be seen as a city of electrons somewhere, a server farm in Norway or anywhere else in the world, but at one physical location, keeping all these bits of data moving, so that again somewhere millions of little LEDs (not phosphors) of a screen, of a tablet, a mobile device, or television are activated and changing their statuses with ONs and OFFs.

The city could be seen as a metaphor for a user interface for all the videos online, maybe even for all the data in the web. The Austrian architect Dietmar Steiner described the city as a user interface:

»All cities of the world are the same. What was it about Andy Warhol and his McDonald's beauty rating? Moscow was not a beautiful city then. According to Laurie Anderson, McDonald's is the symbol of home for Americans because it signals recognizable permanence. In the meantime, Warhol's "beauty" has achieved world dominance, and Laurie Anderson may feel "at home" even in Moscow. The same signs everywhere; Coca-Cola, McDonald's, Benetton, Body Shop, Levis—we know the brands and what they offer the world over, and we know how much more difficult it can be to buy some simple loaf of bread. Apart from that, we live in uniform hotels, follow the same sign codes through airports without ever giving it a thought, and we recognize taxis as taxis everywhere in the world.« (Steiner n.d.)

In every city in the world we recognize the same signs. Even if the city appears as a jungle of signs, we know the trademarks and their worldwide offers. For Steiner Wim Wender's 1991 film *Until the End of the World* is a lecture on sign systems, hotel halls, car insides, phone booths, whose local color on a totally new level creates differences.

How do we know which city is shown in an image, which country? Actually, the sign system creates the differentiation.

The city as a total perception doesn't exist. There is the city as an idea, there are houses; the city has a name, or what will be a city needs a name. The first form of conquering a city is reading its typology and conventions, the systems of rules—here a new layer of interpretation is added. The reading, materially fixed as a user interface, can only be manifested through its own writing of its use and has in principle three levels of approaching. These all are based on the assumption that every experience of a city is a form of conquest.

The first and major form of conquest of a city takes place in the company of a scout or a guide. The arrival in the foreign city is directly channeled. You are expected. The perception will be selected. The stranger will be included in a partial system of the city, which signals security and confidence. The initiation of the user interface of the city follows these instructions. If you go with line X you come to Y, there you find.... don't sit near the driver in the taxi... Where and how you eat and drink, the guide tells you.

The opposite of the guide is the lone wolf as Steiner describes. He is simply the single fighter. He arrives at the airport; he gets his luggage and doesn't know further. There is no one, no info desk, and no assistance. But he finds a sign with hotels on it. He notes the numbers, first the well-known ones, takes a taxi, checks in, decodes the use of hotel telephone, air conditioning, TV, minibar ... he is always in adventure mode. This path cannot be taken without a basic knowledge of the regulation techniques.

The loner in the foreign city needs his learned routine. He follows the learned international sign systems and adapts with failure and pain to the local rituals.

Both models of approach to the user interface of the city lead to the third, which is a mixture of the local guide and the confident stranger, because both experience only a separated and limited part of the city and depend therefore on a preconditioned reception of the potential perception.

Both gain confidence with the rituals of daily life of the city. Now, the user interface bears fruit. Reading stops, abstract signs replace words, building an authentic flair of the place.

The user interface of a city is built up by an image, and a melting point, constructed from things and signs and their directed perception. This user interface is in its production not controllable. The world of signs is the world of power.

MODES OF NAVIGATION

Steiner's three approaches to a city are similar to the modes of navigation as Larry Elin described them in his 2001 book on multimedia design and development: Navigation is how the user moves about through a multimedia product.

Elin differentiates between three general kinds of navigation. The first one is the »browse« mode, in which the user has complete freedom to roam around. The second is the »guided tour« mode, in which the user is led from one node to another. In the third kind, called the »customized« mode, the user self-delimits access to the content by specifying some preferences (Elin 2001, 20).

Staying with multimedia, one of the now classic works of interactive installation comes to mind: *The Legible City* (1988-1991) by Jeffrey Shaw.

In Shaw's installation, visitors sit on a stationary bicycle and *move* through projected streets in front of them. Instead of buildings, the streets are lined by letters and are literally legible.

»On their passage through the city, cyclist-visitors can pursue various narrative threads, accumulating their own history of the city. On a small display on the handlebars is a map of the city on which the cyclists can plot their position. ... A city is simultaneously a tangible arrangement of forms and an immaterial pattern of experiences, says Shaw. Its architecture is a morphology of language, its ground plan a psycho-geographic network and its streets a labyrinth of narrative pathways.« (Media Art Net n.d.)

For Vertov the experience of the city and its *navigable spaces* leads to a dream of a new world. He constructs a camera-eye to disrupt and disorient routine habits of perception and understanding. Cinema sets in place a space and architecture of perception, attention and sociality. The novelty of cinema's navigable spaces lay in the experience of being both here and there. Distant places, places where we were unable to go, come close and open new realms of experience. We *make world* through cinematic spaces and technology.

»Shaw retains a Situationist's view of the softness and fluidity of experience and expanded cinema's agenda of disrupting the usual relations of cinematic spectatorship. He starts from the specificity of the site of reception, and the way it acts on the viewer's body, and then creates environments which are negotiated through perceptual disorientation and physical movement.« (Donald 2003)

In *The Legible City*, Shaw's computer-generated three-dimensional letters form words and sentences to create buildings and streets following the street plans of Manhattan, Amsterdam, or Karlsruhe. »A small screen in front of the bicycle shows a map of each city, enabling the rider to choose whether to ride through Manhattan or Amsterdam or Karlsruhe and to track their progress. The handlebars and pedals of the bicycle are linked to a computer that allows control of direction and speed.« The visitor using the bicycle starts on an imaginary journey through the constructed, but known navigable space of the city. The ride creates a different kind of narrative, a layer on top of the navigable space of the city that becomes a cinematic city that disorients routine habits of perception and understanding, like Vertov did.

Michel de Certeau had pointed out that space is a practiced place: »[T]he street geometrically defined by urban planning is transformed into a space by walkers. In the same way, an act of reading is a space by the practice of a particular place: a written text, i.e. a place constituted by a system of signs« (de Certeau 1984, 97).

De Certeau defines walking as an action »lacking a place«. By means of this action those who traverse the city move their thoughts, emotions, impressions, and projections through the city streets, thus writing its *urban text.* »'Space' is, for de Certeau, a collaboratively created semantic dimension of place « (de Certeau 1984, 103).

»The serious question raised by Flann O'Brien's comedy [*The Third Policeman*]—what navigable spaces have actually (rather than counterfactually) been created through media interfaces, new and old?—is elegantly encapsulated by yet another novelist, Italo Calvino. He recalls how, in his childhood, cinema 'satisfied a need for disorientation, for the projection of my attention into a different space, a need which I believe corresponds to a primary function of our assuming our place in the world'.« (Donald 2003)

As James Donald points out, the space and technology of cinema, like the physical spaces of home and school in the case of the young writer Calvino, act on the body of the viewer to teach him »routines of conduct.« In the imaginary image-loaded world of cinema, the viewer enters at the same time a different space. The cinematic space is one of representation and phantasy. In this mediated space, the viewer becomes subject to the experience of disorientation.

»Calvino's insight provides my hypothesis: that this experience of disorientation can help us to understand the history and consequences of technologically mediated spaces. The flâneur is better understood as a methodological device than as the reconstruction of a historical form of consciousness.« (Donald 2003)

Walter Benjamin had used Baudelaire's flâneur to investigate and cope with the modern metropolis. The flâneur stands for a certain technique of observation and imagination. The metropolis is overwhelming in organizing things, creating and occupying spaces with its imposing technology. The individual, as Benjamin's teacher Georg Simmel points out, cannot maintain itself and is at risk of being crushed by the Golem city. The survival strategy of the metropolitan citizen is an aesthetic of self-creation.

Here Benjamin explores the disciplines of flânerie in three major steps. In the first step, the flâneur creates a distance, a kind of disembodied spectatorial attitude: it is to be in the center of the world but at the same time hidden away, incognito. In the second step, the flâneur domesticates the physical world while processing it as images and narrative. In the third step the flâneur produces knowledge, and then gains control through this knowledge.

»In the flâneur, the joy of watching is triumphant. It can concentrate on observation; the result is the amateur detective. Or it can stagnate in the gaper; then the flâneur has turned into a badaud [stargazer; a mere idler].« (Benjamin 1973, 69)

Simmel had already by 1903 described the everyday experience as being bombarded by rapidly changing images and sharp discontinuities, »unexpectedness of onrushing impressions.« For Benjamin, reality is turned into a spectacle and the subject into a spectator. This created the need for cinema. With cinema the city interior became like a movie and »perception in the form of shocks was established as a formal principle« (Donald 2003).

Movement in the city, observations of people, buildings, streets, objects, and things, and imagination turns into the cinematic apparatus of camera-eye, screen, and moviegoer.

With its virtual presence, television exaggerates and continues to create a new geography. Rudolf Arnheim wrote in 1930:

»So television as a means of spiritual intercourse, proves to be a relative of the car and the aeroplane. ... [L]ike the machines of locomotion that the last century gave us, it alters our relation to reality itself, teaches us to know it better, and lets us sense the multiplicity of what is happening everywhere at one moment." (Arnheim 1936, 279-80)

What television does successfully is simply bringing the world inside people's living rooms. It does this by adapting to the rhythms and routines of everyday live. Actually, it creates the world.

The technologies of television and telephone should be viewed together. What they have in common is a »combination of universality and locatedness. They are both 'global' in their reach and infinitesimally 'local' at the point of reception and use« (Donald 2003; McCarthy 2001, 10). Whereas the cinema offers the imaginative experience of some other space while we watch, television and telephone allow the *virtual* presence of distant people and events. They are both »space-binding« (Weber 1996). Television, especially, allows new forms of meaning-making and builds a new kind of community. It flexibly blends into our everyday environment.

»The secret of television, Anna McCarthy argues, is its adaptability. As a technology, it is site specific. Television's increasingly ubiquitous presence in shopping malls, restaurants, pubs, stores, gyms, doctor's waiting-rooms, airport lounges, planes and trains is then both cause and symptom of a transformation in the nature of those 'public' spaces as profound as any changes to the 'private' space of the home. Even that public/private distinction becomes almost too ambiguous to sustain. These public spaces are mostly privately owned, monitored by private security forces, and closely policed in terms of access and conduct. Still, as Anna McCarthy impatiently observes, there is little point in whingeing that television contaminates the publicness of urban space by 'privatising' it. If cities are becoming ever more like television, she implies, get used to it. This is where we live.« (Donald 2003)

Here the question of how can we watch all the videos produced, uploaded, shared, etc., dissolves into the continuation of mediated spaces, geographies of non-places, uncanny and chaotic social spaces in an over-populated, crowded world of things and people, »thick with images, sounds, words, messages, and stories« (Donald 2003).

Media technologies require us to navigate through worlds of meaning, cities of representations, coded imaginary and thick images. To avoid becoming dizzy, we need to find subjective ways to navigate in a »matrix of perception, attention, movement and belonging« (Donald 2003). That is simply our reality. Simulated life as a player of *Grand Theft Auto* starts aimless driving through Los Angeles, constructing his own reality while stopping here and there, and adapting the space to himself, doing things that wouldn't make sense but make him ready to act in a world already mapped as post-television.

»Where do we make world, make ourselves, make community? It must be where we act as embodied agents but at the same time occupy Calvino's different space, the space of culturally coded information: concretely, in the flâneur's detached observation of the crowd, in the fantasy-spaces of cinema, in the message-saturated space of the home, in the dizzying abstraction of information and communication networks. To get the measure of what it means to live and act in this world Vattimo quotes Nietzsche from *The Gay Science*: to be free means 'continuing to dream knowing one is dreaming.'
It is dreaming as a creative act, as a way of engaging with the world by being out-of-joint with the world. It is dreaming as the exercise of imagination—the mode of thought that Brian Massumi considers 'most precisely suited to the differentiating vagueness of the virtual.' Imagination he also equates with intuition, the 'mutual envelopment of thought and sensation' that we have tracked in our hallucinatory journey from flânerie to surfing.« (Donald 2003)[3]

CONSTRUCTIVE INSTABILITY

For the first *Video Vortex* reader, Thomas Elsaesser went on a journey through (or in) YouTube. Elsaesser begins with the assumption that life looks more like art. What was once the driving force of the historical avant-garde—bringing art closer to life through techniques of montage, collage, assemblage, collision, the combination of seemingly unrelated elements or materials, the practice of »displacement«—has already happened; technological developments, style, *bios* (individual life and its finitude) and *zoe* (natural life with its cycles) as double heteronomy, biological processes available as technologies, threaten art with disappearing. »In other words, 'art' and 'life' are both coming under pressure from external forces, but in such a way that they seem to be mutually refiguring each other« (Elsaesser 2008). The nature/culture divide seems not to exist anymore.

---

3   See also: Massumi (2002), Vattimo (1992).

Elsaesser asks, is it possible to detect modes of being »that [do] indeed cross back and forth between the traditional boundaries of nature and culture, of technology and biology?« (Elsaesser 2008)

He detects three major paradoxes through his experience of YouTube. The first paradox:

»YouTube, as indicated, is a user generated content site, with a high degree of automation, where nonetheless a certain structured contingency obtains, as indicated by the remarkably coherent clusters I was able to extract via the tags attached to the videos. The structured contingency is, then strongly informed and shaped by mathematics, via its programming architecture and design, as well as its search and sort algorithms. At the same time, it seems to mimic certain primitive forms of life, comparable to the swarms and clusters of bacteria (such as in yeast, algae, slime mould or other 'emergent' life-forms), not least because what exists on YouTube is constantly growing, changing and adapting (at a rate of some 60.000 a day, with almost as many removed because they infringe someone's copyright). The site, traversed by a semantic traveller like myself, presents the impression of an organism, alive and in full evolution, where things mutate, accumulate, disperse, die and re-emerge.« (Elsaesser 2008)

The second paradox: a stupid machine and intelligent user-generated tags produce a most varied and interesting cast of characters,

»ways of knowing and ways of being that are lucid and reflexive, educational and participatory, empowering and humbling, in short: marking an unusually soft dividing line between creative design and hard-core engineering, art and technology, singularity and repetition: preconditions if one wants to come to an understanding of the possibility of new 'life-forms' emerging at one of the sites of the post-human: the electronic world of algorithms and statistics, of contingency, constraint and collapse, in short: of constructive instability and performative failure, in a world divided, but also held together by Ranciere's 'double heteronomy'.« (Elsaesser 2008)

The third paradox, then: it is addictive to spend time in or with YouTube.

»Yet after an hour or so, one realizes on what fine a line one has to balance to keep one's sanity, between the joy of discovering the unexpected, the marvelous and occasionally even the miraculous, and the rapid descent into an equally palpable anxiety, staring into the void of a sheer bottomless amount of videos, with their proliferation of images, their banality or obscenity in sounds and commentary. Right next to the euphoria and epiphany, then, there is the heat-death of meaning, the ennui of repetition and of endless distraction: in short, the relentless progress of entropy that begins to suck out and drain away all life.« (Elsaesser 2008)

Elsaesser concludes that what it seems we are faced with is »the uncanny possibility that the avant-garde techniques of the first part of the 20th century, and the 'life' processes of the 21st century reveal important common features, across the medium, the Internet destined to disappear as a medium because of its very pervasiveness and ubiquity« (Elsaesser 2008).

His final conclusion then is that in order to survive, art must become more lifelike than life itself while life is constituted as engineered, programmed and *made*.

MODES OF CHANNELING

While looking at methods and methodologies to cope with the flood of videos around us and following various paths of exploration, it is logical to look at parallels in practices in digital culture like photo-sharing. Susanne Holschbach has conducted an excellent study of Flickr, the photo-sharing universe on the web. In *Framing [on] Flickr* she investigates the process of channeling that drive the flow of pictures into specific paths and control users' access to the pictures (Holschbach 2010). What interests Holschbach about the photo-sharing phenomenon is what takes place between the uploaded pictures and through them. Her view of course is based on a photographic theoretical perspective that would question at first what kind of images are uploaded, how are they presented, and which criteria are used to organize them. As she notes, her research is confronted with the problem of temporary constellations of images and related practices. The permanent process of classification, evaluation, and integration resulting from user activities and program operations resists scientific approaches as the object of interest constantly changes its conditions. The assessment of objects depends on temporary constellations that might not exist later on. Differentiating between channels like amateur photography and stock photography only results in a fragmented inside. Evaluation of the user seems to be based on interestingness; quality of an image is transformed into commodity.

»However, before confirming this comparison by making a moral evaluation of stock photography's access to supposedly "more authentic" snapshots and amateur photographs, one should consider that, on the one hand, the transformation of the fleeting, accidental and casual into an aesthetic of the fleeting, accidental and casual and its capability of being duplicated and reproduced—with the danger of becoming clichéd—is inherent in photography. On the other hand it must be borne in mind that amateur photography and the photographic industry already have a long history of interaction.« (Holschbach 2010)

Problematic and of interest is that the comeback of analog photography—such as found images from flea markets—are grouped as channels. The navigation in the world of Flickr appears interest-controlled and relies on a system of reference, rearrangement, and relabeling, creating an ever-growing archive. The original images are decontextualized through resorting and rebuilding of collections. Holschbach points to Kracauer's reservations about the flood of images threatening to eradicate the possibly existing consciousness of decisive aspects. She points to Susan Sontag noting the creation of stereotypes out of unique objects and vital artistic products out of stereotypes. »Is it not the case that, since the start of digital photography, increasingly dense layers of pictures force themselves between the images of real things?« (Holschbach 2010)

This also suggests Vilem Flusser's view of the person taking the snapshot as an extension of his camera's self-timer, consumed by its greed. The world in Flickr or through Flickr appears as one categorized by »interestingness« and leading toward the continued production of redundant pictures, de-professionalizing and deskilling the art of photography.

»For example, could one take Flickr into account as an instrument that could cope with today's flood of photographic pictures by directing them into the relevant channels and bundling them according to the wide range of interests and, in doing so, not only deepen and broaden the established photographic genres and practices, but also differentiate or undermine these genres and practices: whether by automatic referential structures or 'indisciplined' user behavior. And, not least, Flickr and other platforms are not identical with contemporary photographic practice; they merely refer to this by giving impressive proof that, in the era of its digitalization, photography appears to be more popular and also livelier than ever before.« (Holschbach 2010)

Zooming In

While Holschbach theorizes the channeling of digital photographs and questions various content-related issues pointing to existing academic discourses, Nadav Hocman and Lev Manovich's *Instagram City* or *PhotoTrail* project tries to explore cultural difference with the billions of photographs shared by millions of users of Instagram. Through image mapping and new methods of visualization based in digital humanities and software studies, this project explores visual patterns, dynamics, and structures of social media production.

The *PhotoTrail* project included 2.3 million Instagram photos from 13 cities around the world. The premise was that temporal changes in number of shared photos, their locations, and their visual characteristics could uncover social, cultural and political insights about people's activities around the world (Manovich 2013).

»How are users' experiences of production, sharing, and interaction with the media they create mediated by the interfaces of particular social media platforms? How can we use computational analysis and visualizations of the content of visual social media (e.g., user photos, as opposed to upload dates, locations, tags and other metadata) to study social and cultural patterns? How can we visualize this media on multiple spatial and temporal scales?« (Holchman and Manovich 2013)

Hochman and Manovich examine these questions through first, the Instagram interface and how this interface and the application's tools structure users' understanding and use of the »Instagram medium.« Then they compared the »visual signatures« of 13 different cities through photos shared from these cities.

Illustration 2: Radial image plot of Instagram uploads

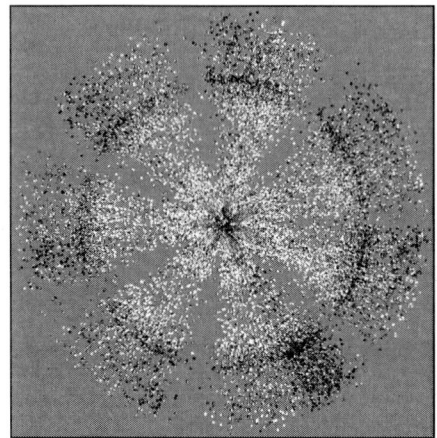

Source: http://firstmonday.org/ojs/index.php/fm/article/view/4711/3698

Finally, the researchers used »spatio-temporal visualizations of over 200,000 Instagram photos uploaded in Tel Aviv, Israel over three months to show how they can offer social, cultural and political insights about people's activities in particular locations and time periods« (Hochman and Manovich 2013).

The researchers follow a strategy of »multi-scale reading« using high-resolution visualizations that show complete image sets to explore metadata and patterns. They also take individual photographs into consideration. »Distant reading« of patterns is combined with "close reading" of particular artifacts through special visualization techniques, such as radial image plotting and image montage. They organize all images in large sets on the basis of visual properties and metadata.

Image manipulation tools, location annotations of photos, and instant sharing were not new to Instagram when the research was conducted in October 2010. What was significant was the operation of these elements in a single mobile application. This might be why Instagram is so widespread and in sync with current cultural trends. Most important to this research is Instagram's presentation of geographical and temporal data in a very specific media environment.

The interface suppresses temporal, vertical structures in favor of spatial connections. The software application privileges space over time. The timestamp of each photo remains in flux. The traditional representation of time is eliminated through an assemblage of images from people we are following. The filters applied in the software suggest another time than the one when the photo was taken, replacing the existing atmosphere with a particular new atmosphere based on social relations.

»The result is a multi-temporal image which suggests at least three different temporal references: the actual time when the picture was taken, the time evoked by a certain filter, and the time span indicated by the application when viewing the photo. Ironically, while a geo-temporal tagged image connotes the precision of time an space coordinates (we know the exact longitude/latitude coordinates together with the exact time it was taken) the software subverts this message by displaying multiple users' photo-streams in a single feed, a relative time indication, and a distorted, filtered photographic image.« (Hochman and Manovich 2013)

There is no specific time for any image. The image becomes timeless or »time-thickened.« We are together in the same time. This is an emerging operative cultural logic. A single element is related to a whole that promises any image from anywhere, similar to Google Earth. Our personal experience shared with the Instagram photo leaves its time boundaries under the efforts of a corporate interest. Google Earth and Instagram confront us »with two distinct ways of seeing: an objective, elevated and fixed form versus grassroots documentation efforts that present spontaneous and highly personal sentiments that inherently reject the technological pursuit of fine details and accuracy of a 'mechanical' (now digital) eye « (Hochman and Manovich 2013).

These logics are now merged. Google lets users add their own geospatial data to the default Google Earth representation. On top of the existing geographical data, another complex media layer is created.

As Hochman and Manovich point out, the operative software logic behind this is simply that an individual is always related to a documentary whole. The tags of a single person are related to everyone's tags. A user's photo is related to all other photos via the shared map or coordinate system. Old and new, local and global, parts and wholes are creatively placed together. Social media emphasizes that space is a social construction.

The specific social experience emphasizes "now," but is carefully curated and edited—photos are not always immediately shared. The meaning of a space results from the integration of spatial, cyclical, and linear (following Henry Lefebvr's rhythm analysis and his temporal understanding of place and space) social timespace.

»Social time and space—as the combination of the cyclical and the linear times in our visualizations—are not only relational (linear) but also historical (cyclical). Our visualized social timespace is thus a representation of an active web of affinities that is constantly shaped and reshaped by users.... Our analysis shows how Instagram's interface superimposes its strong "message" (or "interface signature") on its users, shaping what and how they communicate.... [Our analysis] shows how the proportions between photos with different filters are remarkably similar for all cities. However, when examined on a large scale we can see that social timespace is not universal. As apposed to Instagram's interface uniformity imposed on all application users in all places—in terms of time representation, photo dimensions, same set of filters etc.—we found small but systematic visual differences between photos shared on Instagram in different cities.« (Hochman and Manovich 2013)

Hochman and Manovich's research and visualization shows the visual signature of each analyzed city. All cities exhibit at the same time local, regional, and universal characteristics. Instagram's global shared photo universe still shows cultural difference throughout the world. From global to particular, software tools like Instagram allow a free exploration of single photos while maintaining the ability to instantly shift to a general overview of millions of images. We are not bound by strict sorting categories. While moving from one location or spatio-temporal relation to another, multiple contexts and scales, differences, similarities, or patterns become notable.

Hochman and Manovich emphasize the transition from a web—where users share, comment, and tag—to a web of aggregators, which collects social data. Such aggregators act as »live stream readers.« They provide an algorithmically summarized view. This summarized data allows configuration of dynamic patterns based on attributes like time, place, color, composition, and so on.

»If functions and relations are now more important than purposes, and we are, as previously suggested, encouraged to see ourselves as specific points of time and place, then we are also prompted to think of ourselves as singularities which are part of various wholes, each contributing to a constantly growing database that then needs to be visualized and explored. This is the essence of this new "media paradigm": exploring diversities of singularities not through hierarchies and categories but rather through relations, transitions and sequences, while moving from the singular to the plural, from the close to the distant.« (Hochman and Manovich 2013)

Cultural analytics and methods of visualization as Hochman and Manovich used them in this Instagram research could help us learn to read and understand the experience of multilayered patterns of video. In contrast to a traditional method of defining a small number of genres and categories, such a methodology seems much more useful, as we can follow the algorithmic principle of search engines and try to consider all possibilities, links, features, characteristics, and properties of any given object (Network Cultures 2013). A search engine analyzes every single webpage and generates unique descriptions that consider millions of variables. Interactivity provides a new dimension of culture that was not present when movies where just playing in theaters and television consisted of a limited number of channels and program genres. Following the example of Netflix, categories are temporal and constantly changing. It is becoming more relevant to study how people interact, or how they use a single artifact. Web analytics therefore needs to analyze user interaction with websites over the course of billions of billions of interactive sessions, on various levels on data, practically resulting or referencing the use of frequencies.

Buckminster Fuller used the term *frequency* to specify length and size, allowing for use of the term to describe both geometric systems and events in nature. Fuller points out that frequency never relates to the quantity »one,« for it necessarily involves a plurality of experiences (Edmondson 1987).

A »high-frequency energy event« describes »most tangible structures, which might be popularly thought of as 'solids.'«A good way to illustrate this through a visible image is the white foam of breaking ocean waves. »Upon closer inspection, the apparent continuum of whiteness is a result of an enormous number of tiny clear bubbles, which appear continuous because of their close proximity. This punctuated consistency is analogous to all matter, although most examples are not visible to the naked eye« (Edmondson 1987).

Coming back to Manovich's cultural analytics, the way we use Google Earth is becoming an exemplary way to handle incredible amounts of complex data. The operation of zooming in and out helps to distinguish between various or multiple levels—levels of creator, levels of group, affiliate, paradigms, and practices.

Google Earth from street view to satellite overview is the practical paradigmatic example of zoomability. Zoomability is becoming a characteristic idea of culture embedded in the software and media we use. Searching and finding are outdated ideas of a paradigm of a not too distant past. While we talk about borders softening, genres merging or mashing up, mixing and remixing, Transmedia and other concepts are based on mid-century ideas of existing small boxes, shelves, or categories. We simply need to consider that today's technology generates a description for every single thing, object, file, and document. Instead of finding one particular video on the web, we are confronted with patterns representing variables like shot length, aspect ratio, and so on. Software will automatically detect a video's boundaries. The question then is to look at the insides—the single content of a single object or thing.

Manzara

The Turkish word *manzara* means *view* or *sight*. It also means a place with a particular view when referring to a landscape, which can be seen from a high point or special opening towards a specific scenery.

Now, if video is all around us and we are in a kind of video-scape or video sphere, than the *manzara* or view could be the hunt for a detail or a single point. A single video I am watching on my computer would be my view. It is more important than all the other videos surrounding it, which exist at the same time and even in the same location.

Manzara or this idea of view explains our actual present behavior and relation toward online video. The video in our Facebook timeline is a zoom or micro-view of our surroundings or *Umwelt* (German).

The notion of *Umwelt* is borrowed and goes back to the work of the biologist Jakob von Uexküll (1864–1944). *Umwelt* is the perceptual world in which an animal exists and interacts. »Signifying things trigger chains of events, sometimes spelling the difference between life and death« (Uexküll 2010, 2). Life forms can have different worlds. Their perception differs even they share the same environment. For Uexküll there are as many worlds as sensors or eyes in a specific environment. In other words, our world of perception is not the only one. Thomas Sebeok extended Uexküll's work toward a spiderlike semiotic web in which our understanding of our world is build by our social and personal constructions (Uexküll 2010).

When asked if she thinks Europe and Asia have different concepts of landcape, artist Donna Ong answered:

»I think the biggest difference is maybe the idea of the view. I am not sure whether in modern Asia we have so many views. Going to a mountain to look at a view—I think that could be a Western concept. The way you go to a particular place to look at something, which is deemed beautiful. I think in Asia we are often surrounded by the landscape. It surrounds you and you are in it. It's not too much that you stand apart from it and admire it, but you are within it, working in it. ...
In Singapore in particular, because there is not many views, everything is very detailed and close-up. We tend to look at things close-up, we tend to close things out, spaces are quite small, the flats and things like that. So, we look at things closer. If we think of exhibitions, the size is different or the perspective is different, lower or a different kind of scale. Usually, it is more a micro view, from far away looking down, close-up. As a result, the detail becomes more important. Everything is very tight. I will say just one last thing about landscape from the Asian and Western viewpoints: I think in Asia it is more about things jumbled up together and being tied together, whereas in Western culture, things are more separate and distinct. One looks at things in isolation, separated from others.« (Valvidia Bruch 2013).

Why are Asian video sensor manufactures currently looking into producing 8k or even 16k chips? From a European understanding, do we really need so much more detail in an image or a video? The answer seems again to be a matter of view—in Western culture, overview is related to the concept of story and storytelling, where there's a beginning, a middle, and an end, in contrast to an open story embedded in each detail, developing further in the form of a pattern or a surrounding. This as well reminds of the idea of a surrounding or better Uexkuell's *Umwelt*.

V-BRICKS

> It's simple. People produce works and we do what we can with them. We use them for ourselves.
> SERGE DANEY

> When I receive a new poetic image, I experience its quality of inter-subjectivity. I know that I am going to repeat it in order to communicate my enthusiasm.
> GASTON BACHELARD

BUILDING BRICKS

If you want to build a house, you need a plan. If you have already a bunch of bricks, you'll start to build walls. You'll sort them, then layer the ground, an outline to build on and start the construction. Without a further plan, you will be able to build walls with openings, perhaps a simple roof. At the end you'll have a shed. It will not be very beautiful, but obviously functional.

A plan can make things more complicated for the good. It guides you to more complicated constructions and ways of building. Simple shapes combine to form more complex structures. At this point the simple bricks will not be enough anymore. They need to be in different sizes and volumes to achieve more variations. More variations become more exiting, more creative, more beautiful and lasting. You can spend more time on the work.

A wall builder would select a standard size of brick, cutting them according to the plan if necessary for in-between sizes. He would layer the bricks following the plan, quickly creating a basic construction. This skeleton is then the basis to mount more variables to create different forms and shapes.

With bricks, you can construct real houses; with miniature versions of bricks, you can construct castles, cars, and even space ships. What I am referring to is LEGO.

LEGO was the invention of Ole Kirk Kristiansen, who developed an interlocking brick system through the 1940s that was patented in January 1958. The name comes from the Danish words *leg godt,* meaning, »play well« (coincidentally, this means "I put together« in Latin) (LEGO Group 2011). Playing and combining is the basic concept of LEGO, the company aims to »inspire and develop the builders of tomorrow.«

Playing with LEGO creates a world of imagination and absorption. The bricks fit intuitively together, and construction usually involves males of a family from childhood up to AFOLs (»Adult Fans of LEGO«).[1] »There are approx. 4,000 different elements in the LEGO range—plus 58 different LEGO colors. Each element may be sold in a wide variety of different colors and decorations, bringing the total number of active combinations to approx. 8,000« (LEGO Group 2011).

LEGO today, with its bricks and mini figures, makes it easy for kids to recreate stories, including knights, astronauts, and policemen to branded sets like Star Wars and Harry Potter. Together with films they watched, games they played, books they read, or stories they heard, kids can delve into their own imagination of fantastical worlds by simply combining the little plastic blocks.

»I know that my desire to get into engineering was significantly influenced by my playing with LEGO® as a child. I loved the space sets and recall many, many hours playing with them. I would build something, play with it, change it, play some more, change it again, etc. I was always tinkering with my designs. What I have discovered with my continuing LEGO® play (Technics and Mindstorms get most of my attention now - ...) is that it is process of building something quickly, discovering the strengths and weaknesses of the design, iterating on the design, and tweaking the

---

1   Girls came very late into the view of the company with the marketing of girl-oriented sets in 2012.

best concepts, is the best part. These LEGO® creations draw upon multiple domains: structures, mechanisms, motors, transmissions, pneumatics, sensors, and programming. Development is happening simultaneously across these domains - even if there is more than one person one working on the machine. Everything must be integrated on the machine. This is the ideal multi-domain, collaborative, and agile development environment!« (Loew 2013)

CLIPS

Similar to the little colored bricks of LEGO, digital nonlinear video editing software defines its material as clips. Clips in digital video are the bricks to build sequences and temporal audiovisual events.

A clip has a name; it consists of video, audio, and timecode; it has duration. In its 1998 glossary, AVID Technology Inc. defined a clip as

»1. A segment of source material digitized into your system at selected IN and OUT points and referenced in a project bin. The clip contains pointers to the media files in which the actual digital video and audio data is stored.
2. In a record in a log, which stands for one shot, the clip includes information about the start and end timecode for the shot, the source tape name, and the tracks selected for editing.
3. In OMFI, a general class of objects in the OMF Interchange class hierarchy representing shared properties of source clips, filler clips, attribute clips, track references, timecode clips, and edge code clips. A clip is a subclass of a component.
See also master clip, media files, subclip.« (AVID 1998).

When you do a video recording, you define a start and an end by pressing the record button. On the recording device, a timecode starts running either from 0 or from the actual timestamp of the device. The recorded moving image is stored as a digital video signal somewhere. This means that analog information entering through the lens is scanned, read out, and converted to digital information. This individual recording is a clip. It's a source with a defined volume.

The clip is an object or an entity, a stored signal with a beginning and end, mainly defined through its duration and its audiovisual content.

A clip is not a *shot* and a clip is not the smallest or *minimal unit* of video. A clip can be split into smaller units used for building meanings. A sequencing or an assemblage of clips could create a meaningful sequence or event as well; thus, semantically the clip is not necessarily a singular element.

A clip is a video object; if it is not split, it is supposed to be trimmed, its edges, head, and tail shortened. Any application that can record video offers the option of trimming the length by removing frames from the beginning and the end, graphically and visually presenting a fragmented or partial sequence of the images in reference to the clip. The ability to trim any clip from its edges suggests that the clip itself is always rough and imprecise; it needs to be processed to its proper, subjective length. It is an option. This option helps delay the sharing of a recording.

Splitting a clip creates subclips. Once a clip exists somewhere, every activity related to it is a matter of playback. It can be played back as a whole, but it also can be played back in endless variations of smaller units till by definition the technical smallest element of a video in a nonlinear editor is the frame. The number of frames defines the amount of playback possibilities. A subclip is an instruction by the user to play only part of the clip after virtually trimming head and tail.

In some sense, a frame could be a minimal unit, but the frame itself and its content can again be atomized in millions of semantic elements, points, and so on.

In *Language and Cinema*, Christian Metz discusses the problem of the *minimal unit*:

»It is even more important to underline the fact that the theme of the minimal unit, in discussions of cinematic semiotics, is often based on a tacitly asserted idea, which is precisely the one which calls for the most severe criticism—namely, the idea that there would exist in the cinema one (one single) minimal unit, and that it would thus be associated with all presentations of the big screen. One finds here, in a new form, the confusion between code and language (abstract system and material of expression).... A minimal unit—or a specific type of articulation integrating several units each of which is, in its place, minimal, for example the distinctive unit and the meaningful unit in the linguistic conception of 'double articulation' (Andre Martinet)—is never what is characteristic of a language, but always of a code. No minimal unit (for specific systems of articulation) exists in the cinema: such a unit exists only in each cinematic code.« (Metz 1974, 184-185)

The clip can be seen in relation to a recording as a physical or automated act to initiate the process of storing a real-world scene in the form of a digitized electronic moving image signal.

Why not borrow a term from the world of cinema and call a clip *a shot*? The answer is simple: Because it is from the world of cinema. A shot indicates a clear direction, an intention. It is defined in the narrative world of Hollywood. The act of shooting suggests the construction of a planed process, an intention. It is the intention of constructing a narrative form, an assemblage of hierarchical items, called shots. *Clip* includes an openness. A direction is not defined. A narrative intention is not (yet) embedded. The clip does not know a hierarchy in its first instance. The clip points more to the character of the single recording, the single piece of life, that happened to be in front of the camera. The act of *clipping* is the act of recording, making an image, here a moving image, more or less randomly. Clipping is like taking away a piece of the real and keeping it to be shared or repeated on demand.

In Rudolf Arnheim's film theory, a shot is a perception of the eye (Arnheim 1957). It has a beginning and an end, a running time, and a successive movement of frames, a series of frames running uninterrupted. For Arnheim a *shot*, as well as perspective, is a *tool* for formation. The shot *extracts* significant detail and through this builds an explicit meaning. In filmmaking, every shot has a minimum time, a selected content, explicit movement, defined size, and a context that underlies the rules of visual and graphical composition. Each shot contributes to the plot, the cinematic storytelling purpose.

In the case of online video, cinematic terminology is always at hand and embedded, since video, in its development out of television, inherited these similarities. But when I record a video with my mobile phone and post it on the web, that is not necessarily shooting or filming in the sense of an intentional cinematic approach. In this matter, the more neutral technical software term *clip* is more appropriate.

Of interest in the AVID definition is the third point: »a clip is a subclass of a component.« AVID already points to another layer implied by technology and defines the clip on the level of program and software exchange. As an object in a program, the clip is part of what is defined as a »class.« A class in object-oriented programming is a template for creating objects, which provides initial values for states or variables of members of a program cast and implementations of behavior as functions of a member. In other words, a class is a template definition of the methods and variables in a particular kind of object, or very simplified it is used to describe one or more objects. Subclasses can inherit all or only some of the characteristics of classes.

»Several programming languages support classes, including Java, C++, Objective C, and PHP 5 and later. While the syntax of a class definition varies between programming languages, classes serve the same purpose in each language. All classes may contain variable definitions and methods, or subroutines that can be run by the corresponding object. ... Classes are a fundamental part of object-oriented programming. They allow variables and methods to be isolated to specific objects instead of being accessible by all parts of the program. This encapsulation of data protects each class from changes in other parts of the program. By using classes, developers can create structured programs with source code that can be easily modified.« (Techterms 2011)

Layering bricks, building complex objects like in LEGO, is possible by applying sets of rules to clips of video. These can be based on Eisenstein's principles of montage, but they don't have to be. As the clip is part of a process, the assemblage of clips is open to various forms of manipulation, processing, which does not necessarily mean to align clips and subclips in linear sequences to output a combined new object—AVID calls it a sequence, and Apple calls it an event. Editing video, unlike editing film, is more related to processing the material instead of just applying a set of combination rules or montage principles.

SERIOUS PLAY

Connecting the LEGO experience with video takes away the force of constructing linear narratives and channeling creativity through assembling shots or clips; instead, it directs our attention more to playful imaginative creation as the purpose of recording video. Assembling a linear narrative can be a playful imaginative process, but recording a clip does not need to have this single purpose. The clip is open to multiple possibilities of usage.

Playing with video, like playing with LEGO, activates the imaginary. As an activity, it consumes time and space, follows technical rule sets like in games, is set in agreed-on conventions, and is not controlled by an authority. A narrative would be another kind of authority. In combining clips with other clips, with subclips, and with elements like text and sound, learning takes place—not just learning to operate a device, but through instant feedback it's learning creating variations of meaning or meaningful variations, following an accumulation of what becomes knowledge.

IMAGINATION

Humans have the unique ability to »form images« or to »imagine.« We use our imagination, our view of an inner image, when we describe something, what we have seen, experienced, done, or dreamed of. Imagination is also creating something and challenging something. »I shall suggest here that a radically new type of imagination is emerging, and that it is about to change us. To sustain this, I shall define *imagination* as the faculty to make and to decipher images« (Flusser n.d.).

For Vilem Flusser, everything that is conceivable will become imaginable, so everything what we can perceive is becoming imaginable. Science, politics, philosophy, aesthetics and theology are creating images. A universe of imaginary concepts will change us. We are not the receivers of images to discover their meanings; we will be using images to produce meaning.

»Images are mediations between man and his world, a world that has become inaccessible to him immediately. They are tools to overcome human alienation: they are meant to permit action in a world in which man no longer lives immediately but that he faces.... The purpose of images is to mean the world, but they may become opaque to the world and cover it, even substitute for it. They may come to constitute an imaginary world that no longer mediates between man and the world, but, on the contrary, imprisons man. Imagination no longer overcomes alienation, but becomes hallucination, or double alienation.« (Flusser 1983)

Danny's Mind

Imagination is a claim very close to the combination of extreme sports and wearable action cameras. Born in 1985, Danny MacAskill is one of the best bike riders in the world. In summer 2013 the energy drink company Redbull published his trial biking project *Danny MacAskill's Imaginate* on YouTube (Red Bull 2013).

Imaginate is promoted as a journey into the mind of Danny. Much like family films, Disney movies, or the phantasies of Peter Jackson, in the opening shot we see a landscape in the early evening close to the magic hour. It follows a cut to a close traveling shot over a small riverbed, accompanied by the sound of water. In another traveling shot behind a lake, we see a white house standing alone in nature, very romantic. A traveling shot on a window. The camera moves onto it. The inside looks warm, and is composed in color contrast to the bluish dark outside. A boy playing with a cyclist figure moves in from the left, plays behind the window, and moves to the right while the camera moves onto a sticker on the glass bearing the title logo of the clip, »Red Bull / MacAskill's Imaginate / Enter Danny's Mind,« combined with a small graphical animation of a cyclist doing a jump and turn over the logo.

Cut inside: music opens on a boy playing with blocks on the floor of his room, building a handicap for his cyclist figure. Close-ups of him, close shot of the figure, close-up of him, cut to the real Danny MacAskill in the constructed phantasy world. Intercutting between extreme close-ups of the boy's eyes and details of the cyclist and his bike. A tilt up on Danny. He raises his head and turns to the imaginative boy, nodding his head. The ride begins.

The video *Inspired Bicycles – Danny MacAskill April 2009* brought him worldwide fame (Inspired Bicycles 2009). The video constructs a simple narrative of an exercising biker as a framework; it is more or less a collection of street trials in and around Edinburgh at various times over a period of a few months. With the underlying song *The Funeral* by Band of Horses, the video creates an adequate, smooth atmosphere to some explicit bike-riding shots, demonstrations of technical difficulties and imaginative, exiting city rides and artistic stunts. In April 2009, this is a video that seems to push the boundaries of trials biking. As a video itself, it is much rougher, with variations in technical and aesthetic shooting quality. Danny's flatmate

Dave Sowerby shot the video. The shots have a spontaneity and originality, giving authenticity to the trials.

Imaginate is like a classically styled, narrative music video promoting a sports act. It reflects in every frame its professionalism. The song "Runaway" by Houston supports and emphasizes the sportive action and creates the atmosphere of the lonely hero and his quest to overcome increasing levels of difficulty. Stylistically, *Imaginate* combines a movie-like introduction with the framework of a story and the style of a music video to promote the Australian energy drink brand Red Bull. The description of the video includes this promotional text: »Experience the world of Red Bull like you have never seen it before. With the best action sports clips on the web and YouTube exclusive series, prepare for your 'stoke factor' to be at an all time high« (Red Bull 2013).

The world Red Bull is already a world of extremes. In October 2012, Red Bull was the sponsor of Felix Baumgartner's space jump, which created a super bubble of likes, shares, and millions of tweets.

ACTIVATE SUIT AND CHEST PACK CAMERAS

On January 31, 2014, camera manufacturer GoPro publishes *GoPro: Red Bull Stratos—The Full Story* on YouTube. GoPro and RedBull go hand in hand with their promotion around extreme human activity suitable for the producer of an energy drink and the manufacturer of an action camera. The suit of Felix Baumgartner was equipped with multiple GoPro Hero 2 cameras pointing in all possible directions to record live video above, below, and at the sides of Baumgartner, to follow the action of the jump in multiple phases. More than a year later, the jump is not only celebrated as an historical event, it is also newly staged with footage from various camera positions not released before.

In October 2012, a single video from some of the live footage by the attached GoPro cameras had already created extreme Twitter activities, commentaries, appreciations, astonishment, and curiosity. The dive itself followed by cameras in the air and on the ground gives little excitement, as a small dot or blip of light rushes down to earth, too fast and too small to stick in the minds of viewers. The dot at the horizon of the fall is like an event not seen or not experienced and therefore not yet believed. The webcast instead amplifies the event and every frame stretches its length and duration. The web in October 2012 played the role television did in 1969 with the moon landing. It brought the event close to the viewing audience on their computers or mobile devices, overcoming the incredible distance of the jump.

Much like television, it sets the scene for the digital event. As it is taking place on the web, it becomes part of the endless universe of the web jukebox and can be repeated over and over, relived again and again. The temporary and single event lives forever. The programming is classic, reenacting television style and practice; the only difference is the camera positions and unbelievable angles to be expected of GoPro. The limited interactive features of YouTube's player still allow the user to replay any moment of interest of the event and its video, depending on network speed and video feed by the servers (Stableford 2012).[2]

Because the web keeps everything, the video will remain in the jukebox. But just a little more than a year later, the release of more camera angles documents what the promotion is aiming at. The video and the extreme sport activity create carefully set in-scene length, extending product exposure beyond the possibilities of television while maintaining the narrative, gaining new users and spreading the ever-fresh story. Although we talk about the web creating attention deficits and short attention spans, the web itself creates longer attention spans through repetitive dramaturgy, applying methods, techniques, and styles from traditional media outlets. It is simply professional advertisement.

The matter of involvement and time is already embedded in the constructed stories of sporting events. As sport suggests and embeds practice over and over again, these videos are always prepared and shot over long time spans. In the case of the jump, the main event is very short but is nevertheless long enough to create endless meaningful material, which can be combined brick by brick to create new narrative possibilities and constructions. The promotional text for *Imaginate* tells us that the video was shot over more than 18 month. It took three weeks to gain 4 million views

---

2   Felix Baumgartner jumps - http://www.youtube.com/watch?v=5eVjhQXRDa4

(Danny MacAskill 2015). The web release strategy, which published it first as a trailer and then in five episodes, aims at involvement with the brand Danny.

The extended narrative of Baumgartner's jump through GoPro's release of another video not only adds freshness with new shots but also opens up another narrative frame. It places the jump in a historical order of space jumps by using archival films of a 58-year-old balloon test jump. The extended description of the jump in the original black and white archive footage presented smaller inside the HD frame of the new video surrounded by black is intercut with a precise demonstration of the moments just before the jump, the initiation of all the cameras, and then the loosing of the connections to the space capsule. The event is reenacted, and not just refreshed, historically categorized, but also absolute present and fresh.

Go Action

In the early 1990s, lightweight television cameras attached to Formula One raising cars became common. With these, along with fly cams over stadiums, remote controlled cranes, and tracking devices at racing tracks, new perspectives in sports programs were added, enriching the television experience and keeping the audience involved in the action by bringing the action up close. In the mid 2000s, out of a desire by enthusiasts to get closer to sporting action and to capture professional-quality images with camera equipment and accessories at affordable prices, the development of small attachable action cameras began. As of this writing, one of the most versatile camera choices is GoPro's high-definition cameras for extreme action video photography. GoPro cameras are light-weight, rugged, wearable, and mountable—on everything from the outside of a plane to the human body. It's the camera of choice for recording skiing, surfing, hunting, and other experiences where a professional, heavy, and expensive camera, or even a smartphone, would be unwise or impossible.

GoPro started selling its first 35mm sports camera in 2005, a »reusable wrist camera« that was small (64 by 76 mm), light (200 g), and waterproof to 5 meters (GoPro 2015). Since then the cameras have evolved: they went digital in 2007 and steadily added storage capacity and screen resolution, to their current (2013) configuration of fixed-lens HD video cameras with a

170-degree angle, built-in Wi-Fi, and frame rates up to 120 fps (Anderson 2013).

The camera is made to create extreme or unusual angles and perspectives, subjective point of views of extravagant and difficult rides, and sharing of the recorded clips to enthusiastic communities online. It recreates unusual angles and perspectives that human beings would be unable to see during the action.

The use and popularity of the action camera suggests that Dziga Vertov's Kino-Glaz (Cine-Eye) has finally become available to be everyone's eye. Vertov saw the Cine-Eye as superior to human eyes. The eye sees very poorly compared with the movie camera, which for Vertov was invented to penetrate deep into the visible world, to explore and record as a memory device. It sees what we don't see.

»The kino-eye lives and moves in time and space; it gathers and records impressions in a manner wholly different from that of the human eye. The position of our bodies while observing or our perception of a certain number of features of a visual phenomenon in a given instant are by no means obligatory limitations for the camera which, since it is perfected, perceives more and better. We cannot improve the making of our eyes, but we can endlessly perfect the camera.« (Vertov 1985, 15)

Vertov expands on this notion:

»I am kino-eye, I am a mechanical eye. I, a machine, show you the world as only I can see it. Now and forever, I free myself from human immobility, I am in constant motion, I draw near, then away from objects, I crawl under, I climb onto them. I move space with the muzzle of a galloping horse, I plunge full speed into a crowd, I outstrip running soldiers, I fall on my back, I ascend with an airplane, I plunge and soar together with plunging and soaring bodies. Now I, a camera, fling myself along their resultant, maneuvering in the chaos of movement, recording movement, starting with movements composed of the most complex combinations.

Freed from the rule of sixteen-seventeen frames per second, free of limits of time and space, I put together any given points in the universe, no matter where I've recorded them.

My path leads to the creation of a fresh perception of the world. I decipher in a new way a world unknown to you.« (Vertov 1985, 18)

Vertov's 1929 film *The Man with a Movie Camera* summed up what he had hoped to achieve with the camera and montage: formally a kind of city symphony, abstract and matching the rhythm of a city during a normal day, intercut with the process of moviemaking. The camera itself is part of the narrative, moving the film forward while it moves around the city, creating extreme exciting shots like being run over by a train, or dazzling superimpositions.

DOGS, EAGLES, FALLS & PIGS

In 1926 Vertov wrote:

»Every instant of life shot unstated, every individual frame shot just as it is in life with a hidden camera, 'caught unawares,' or by some other analogous technique—represents a fact recorded on film, a film-fact as we call it. A dog running by on the street is a visible fact even if we don't catch up with it to read what's written on its collar." (Vertov 1985, 57)

GoPro's famous single clips have a kind of Vertovian approach in their content and execution. They are clips with a defined physical length from a camera positioned and then started before the action; they end shortly after the action and are released in a slightly trimmed version at some later point on some platform. They are not just an action, they are a moment of life as it is, through instant replay relived, through web replay lived by anyone. We are curious, and through our curiosity we are becoming part of the recorded experience.

A typical clip is another video from the partnership between GoPro and Red Bull: Kelly McGarry's October 2013 backflip on a mountain bike over a 72-foot canyon during the Red Bull Rampage 2013. YouTube lists in February 2014 more than 16 million views and 5,000 comments (GoPro 2013a). In the clip, which starts after the GoPro promotion slate, we're at the start of a mountain bike ride. The camera is mounted to Kelly McGarry's helmet. We hear his breathing, the counting, motor sounds. We see the front of the bike, the small grade, and the depth to the left and the right of the path. Kelly is counted to start, and starts. During the ride, we are left with the single GoPro view, the path, his breathing, the shakes. We are in the rider's seat. This is similar to the subjective or first-person camera in a game simulation, but the difference is that this is real. We are with the rider every single second, at the border and at the limit, unsafe, insecure and moving quickly forward over uneven, difficult ground. In January 2014, a YouTube viewer wrote *GTA 5* in a comment, referencing the action adventure video game *Grand Theft Auto* in its fifth release.

It is interesting to go through the comments on the video to follow the amazement the ride has inspired. Several commenters recommend viewing the video full screen. Connie H. wrote, »Awesome!! We are talking beautiful visual and being within the moment. Not real - but experiencing it:))« And Kene Ovenshire made a more detailed and seemingly professional comment in February 2014:

»There are a few parallels here to correctly engaging our horse - look at how relaxed and soft his hands are. He's on a 'loose' handle bar, errrr, rein! But serious, for him to successfully navigate THAT ride his shoulders are back, his weight is back, he's 'driving' off the rear end, and he's 'allowing' flawless guidance to flow through him with minimal "directional control" to the front end, he's balanced at the fulcrum, when he's in the air I promise his pelvis is tipped forward, he maintains a loose rein, his chin is tucked and in alignment with his belly-button, his hips are supple and engaged, he's focused on where he intends to go, he's holding a positive picture of 'I am enjoying this ride and arriving safely at the bottom!!,' and for the amount of adrenaline that MUST be pumping through his body during this ride you can hear his breathing remains very close to measured!! THE PART I CELEBRATE MOST - when he arrives at the bottom of the mountain he is full of gratitude, not ego!! That's cool as shxt! Again, 'Hats- off' Kelly McGarry!! :)))!! You da' MAN!!« (GoPro 2013a)

The most amazing stunt in the ride was Kelly's flip over the 72-foot-long canyon. The ride earned Kelly McGarry a second-place finish in the Red Bull Rampage 2013.

»Camera falls from a sky diving airplane and lands on my property in my pig pen. I found the camera 8 months later and viewed this video« (Munselle 2014).

Another video created a huge amount of shares in early 2014 and went viral on the web. The video shows the recording of a body-mounted GoPro.

It's a subjective view out of the open door of an airplane in the air. We see the open door and are taking part in or follow a preparation for a jump. Suddenly the camera comes loose and falls; the horizon turns and turns. The glitch image is visually very attractive and keeps you watching. And then the camera lands; a pig approaches, and its mouth opens onto our view. The image becomes almost black. Somehow we are in fear of getting eaten, but the pig is unable to pick up the small camera.

By February 24, 2014 the video has 12 million views and more than 3,000 comments on YouTube. The video is immediately met with disbelief. Did this really happen? After the uploader, Mia Munselle, explains that she found the camera eight months later, the mystery builds. YouTube commenters weigh in:

»This has gotta be fake. That far and it lands perfectly straight up and still recording? Seems highly unlikely.« »I shouldn't have watched this on fullscreen. I'M GETTING EATEN BY A PIG.« »THIS LOOKS SHOPPED I CAN TELL FROM SOME OF THE PIXELS AND FROM SEEING QUITE A FEW SHOPS IN MY TIME!!!!!« »Fake! How On Earth Did They Know That It Will Land On A Pig Pen And If They Did Know, Wouldnt They Take A Little Longer Time To Stop The Video? They Are Still On Air! And- A Pig Cant Press Buttons So How Would the Camera Stop Videoing?« (Munselle 2014).

The action camera's clips are recorded from positions and in instances we cannot be in or we might not experience the possibility for ourselves. The clip could be the product of editing, as it follows the narrative that the action camera as object or device has created or is part of. The clip could be edited as long as it is possible that that what we see has really happened and is happening. It becomes true when it is replayed. The clip might be »fake« when it was created, but it becomes real through its existence. It is possible that the camera did not fall into the pigpen. It is possible that the sequence is manipulated. The sequence appears in three phases—the plan, the fall, and the pigpen. The transitions seem plausible.

»Some viewers, however, have speculated that the clip is fake by claiming the camera doesn't meet terminal velocity and that, based on the height it fell from then the speed is wrong« (Moran 2014).

Another popular video in 2013 was from the point of view of an action cam attached to the back of a flying eagle. Again millions shared the video, and again the question of »fake« appeared in the comments on the web.

»In the clip, which is entitled 'Flying eagle point of view', the eagle swoops over stunning ice-lined valley and the snow capped mountains, which rise steeply either side. Since the video appeared on YouTube on Monday, viewing figures have sky-rocketed. On Wednesday afternoon, the clip already had over 100,000 views.
For now, the author of the video remains unknown, but until then we can only watch and admire.« (Inge 2013)

Similar shootings had already been done years before in animal documentaries. A BBC wildlife video uploaded on YouTube in March 2009 demonstrates miniature cameras and their usage to document bird flights and birds' subjective views (BBC Worldwide 2009).

A dog's busy daily life is the main visual source for Johnny Neon's *Hearts* music video (Berkowitz 2012). The filmmaker Dave Meinert had put together a custom rig for his GoPro camera and fixed it on the back of the dog.

»My friend asked me to look after his dog for the weekend« says Meinert, a commercial director and filmmaker.

»I was researching putting a camera on the edge of space so I had a small GoPro camera with me for the weekend (I have recently done this for another video which got released this week too. The end sequence is the camera going up 78,000 feet.) I was walking the dog and the idea came to me. At the same time, another close friend of mine asked me to start thinking about concepts for a video for him. Everything just unfolded.« (Berkowitz 2012)

Meinert says he was going to make a video just to prove to his friend that he did actually take the dog for a walk, but the reactions from onlookers made him take another look.

»'I found an old soccer shin guard in my garage and cut it in half and pop-riveted it to a dog's H-harness,' says Meinert. 'Then I secured the camera on to that by counter-sinking screws into the GoPro base plate and securing them to the shin guard. For the dog lovers out there, know that Lemon absolutely loved it. She got excited whenever she saw the harness. Young dogs like the security of something wrapped around them like this in the same way babies liked to be swaddled in a blanket.'« (Berkowitz 2012)

A final note on action cams and GoPro videos: a fireman rescues an unconscious kitten from a burning house in a 2013 video (GoPro 2013b). The video is edited, but it is clear that it was just shortened and that we are following a real event. The fireman enters the house and walks around. He finds the little kitten on the floor, shows it to his colleague, picks it up, and goes outside. He lays the kitten on the asphalt and puts an oxygen mask on it. The kitten revives. The whole clip is scored with the Dexter Britain song *Perfect Moment*.

The fireman rescues the kitten for us. He sees for us and he has done the thing we would feel morally obligated to do. The rescue is not just any rescue of any kitten by any fireman. It is our walk in and our deep urge to do this morally right thing. The underlying music triggers emotional involvement and empathy. When the kitten takes a breath, we are relieved; this simple act gives us the illusion that the world can be better than wherever we are and whatever we do.

The magic of the action camera is that it becomes our remote eye. It is an edited experience, and thus we could suggest that if it is edited then it is somehow a staged experience. It is magic closer to life. It becomes live as it finds affect in the extraordinary and the exclusive in replaying the video.

CAMERA UNCHAINED

The action camera brings back the very instant of the birth of cinema. It recalls Méliès' attraction to sensationalism. As he tried to demonstrate with his images, we do not want to see a wave; we want to see a wave bigger than any we can imagine—we want to see a storm, a tsunami. As in the early days of cinema, the action camera reproduces actualities, events, and perspectives from the everyday in a sensational manner. What created the curiosity of seeing something for the first time from faraway places in the early days of cinema is the same curiosity that makes us want to see something from an impossible position or perspective. The length of the clip stands in for the length of the ride. It's related to cinema's long take as a narrative device.

The following might seem commonplace in the opening of a movie: The camera is in an elevator riding down to the hotel lobby; the elevator door opens, and the camera moves through the lobby toward the revolving doors. The shot is the opening of F.W. Murnau's 1924 film *The Last Laugh*. To accomplish a tracking shot like this, the cameraman Karl Freund sat on a bicycle and had the camera tied to his torso while someone pushed the bicycle out of the elevator and through the lobby to the outside entrance. With this movement, the camera introduces us to the richness and luxury of the hotel and brings us to the hero, the doorman (played by Emil Jannings) with his impressive bushy mustache and his uniform, »an absurdly ornate long coat adorned with a wealth of brass buttons, a mighty collar, and swooping gold braids on the shoulders« (Tobias 2008). The film is the story of the doorman's downfall.

Although the film is not as famous as Murnau's 1922 *Nosferatu* or the 1927 *Sunrise*, it is remarkable in its use of the camera and cinematic technique. The team of Murnau, the writer Carl Mayer, and the cameraman Karl Freund might have arguably created one of the most important stylistic and formal innovations of 20th-century cinema in this film. The cinematography of *The Last Laugh* »set[s] the stage for some of the most commonly used cinematic techniques of modern contemporary cinema« (Stanjek 1987). The camera moves in more than 40 shots—not just panning, tilting, or tracking, but roving, shaking, and taking the subjective view of the doorman. It is an attempt to expand the language of cinema through the expressive qualities of the camera (Rahul 2008). This technique of the moving camera used in this film was called »die entfesselte Kamera« or »unchained camera« (Unchained Camera Technique 2013).

Whereas the camera was more or less static before 1924, restricted to pans, tilts, and movement attached to moving objects like cars or trains, with this film the camera started to move freely through space, becoming subjectively exploring and being. Freund's cinematographic technique makes the camera part of the narrative process. His camera work has influenced all following films and filmmakers and directors until the present. Abel Gance's 1927 film *Napolean*, Alfred Hitchcock's films of the 1930s, and Orson Welles' 1941 *Citizen Kane* are only a few milestones in film history influenced by Murnau and Freund.

Of course, long camera movement had been explored before, such as in D.W. Griffith's 1916 *Intolerance*, but it was not as expressive as in Murnau's film. Murnau was a student of the German Austrian theater director Max Reinhardt and had intensively studied the theatrical space. Screenwriter Carl Mayer, according to Paul Rotha, had already written camera movements in the script of the 1921 German film *Scherben* for »inherent script purposes.« Rotha characterizes Mayer as follows:

»To look at, he was like Beethoven, but with a more sensitive, a more fragile face. In comparison with his small body (he was about 5 ft. 2 ins.) his head seemed unnaturally big. He would stroll along almost meandering as if blown here and there by the wind. You never knew where you would meet him next. In little cafes in Soho, … on a park bench, in a book shop.... He endeared all people to him; his nurses during his illness, barmen in pubs, caretakers. He had a habit rare in cities of saying 'Good morning' to everyone, whether he knew them or not, … This devotee of the big cities, who 'first made the camera move for inherent script purposes,' … was animated by Dickens' love of aimless vagabondage, his sympathetic concern with cobblestones and stray souls alike the very impulses which prompt the camera itself into action.« (Kracauer 1947, 257)

Georges Sadoul notes that Mayer had written continuous changing angles through combinations of camera movement for another film called *Sylvester*. (Sadoul 1982) For *The Last Man,* the producer and chief of UFA productions Erich Pommer had demanded that Murnau invent »something mad.« Murnau, so it is told, said that one shot would not be enough. He would need something more intensive.

Murnau demanded from Freund[3] a totally freely moving camera. Only this would serve the artistic purposes of the film's narrative. With Mayer's writing and Freund's excellent handling, the camera became a psychological tool. Among the high points of German Expressionism is the shot of a drunken Emil Jannings standing frozen in front of a sliding, lurching camera.

---

3 About Karl Freund see also Film Zeit (n.d.) and Entfesselte Kamera (2013).

The French director Marcel Carne was excited after seeing the film: »On a wagon set, the camera glided, rose, floated or crept in everywhere, where the plot demanded it. She remained no more conventionally on a tripod, she became a person acting in the drama« (Weihsmann 1994).

Murnau, Mayer, and Freund extended the language of film and created a development that, according to Georges Sadoul, is as important as the development of sound. The film explicitly shows how the camera structures the depth of the depicted spaces through its movement. The various traveling shots build up spaces as well deconstructing them. The falling and growing lines in these scenes help the expressionist approach.

Murnau himself comes close to a complex theory of mis-en-scene. He explains the camera movement as follows: »All this leads to a symphony of body and spatial rhythms, the game of mere motion, active and generous. All this is possible if the camera is freed from its inertia (matter)« (Bacher 1978, 11-12)[4]

The camera constructs and deconstructs, builds tension and releases it. With a freely moving camera, Murnau aims to construct a mobile space. This mobile space becomes a neutral space, which can adapt to every kind of creation. He wants to execute the "melodie" of a film through camera movement and therefore creates a cinematic art that frees itself from the fixed conditions of architecture and theater. Formal expression supports the narrative; form becomes content. »For me the camera represents the eye of a person, through this mind you see the action on the screen ... The camera must spin and co curious from place to place changing as moveable as thoughts are « (Bacher 1978).[5]

This emphasis on the camera, and reference to the camera as an eye is very characteristic of the 1920s. Dziga Vertov writes, »In the face of the machine we are ashamed of man's inability to control himself, but what are we to do if we find the unerring ways of electricity more exciting than the disorderly haste of active people«; and, as cited before, «I am an eye. I am a mechanical eye. I, a machine, I am showing you a world, the likes of which only I can see.«

---

4   Translation from German is mine.
5   Translation from German is mine.

Vertov believed that the concept of *Kino Eye* would help man evolve from a flawed creature into a higher, more precise form. Similar to Murnau, Vertov believed film was too *romantic* and *theatric* because of the influence of literature, theater, and music, and that these psychological film-dramas »prevent man from being as precise as a stop watch and hamper his desire for kinship with the machine« (Dziga Vertov 2014).

While Vertov's camera eye was a technical combination of the camera and editing (montage) to create this higher being (as executed in *Man with a Movie Camera*) and therefore in the Russian tradition of montage, Murnau's attempt with his *unchained* camera is clearly a move toward the mobile mise-en-scene and the long take. Murnau pushes film closer to reality. According to French critic Andre Bazin, the meaning of images derives from the attention of the spectator (Monaco 2009). Montage as emphasized by Vertov and Eisenstein rules out ambiguity of expression. The long take and the moving camera create a reality of space that cannot be denied. The film form is intimately involved with spatial relationships, and that is mise-en-scene in other words, the imprint of the director's cinematic vision. In a theory of the long take and the moving camera, cinema becomes a systematic process, a cinema of becoming that exists in a gap between reality and mentality between perfect registration and pure conceptualization between theories of Bazin and Eisenstein. According to David George Menard, »Eisenstein represents reality (i.e. reality is manipulated as art remains a pure construct), that is, reality is taken to art; Bazin presents reality (i.e. it is the art that changes and never the reality), in other words, art is taken to reality« (Menard 2009).

Today the term *unchained camera* is unnecessary because the autonomy of the camera became a standard part of the film language tool set, a fixed inventory since the victory of the MTV style and the hunger of television advertisements for invention. It's standard to have action cameras mounted on anything that moves or set in movement to create dynamic and tension with incredible camera travels, fast tilts, zooms, bullet time, gliding *steadycam* movements, and *jib* cranes for any kind of depiction of scenery. Still, most well-known film directors inside Hollywood and outside use the moving camera because of its spatial qualities, its reality of space as a narrative element. Gaspar Noé's 2002 film *Irreversible* seemingly continues Murnau's tradition by keeping the camera continuously moving while being outside the story, the characters, and their movements, becoming a narrative string and creating another level of cinematic vision. Somehow the compulsion to avoid cutting reminds us of Hitchcock's 1948 film *Rope*. Hitchcock's only limitation was the length of his film stock, so he needed to *close the can* (film slang for changing reels). *Irreversible* didn't need to close any cans, as the camera is free floating with the action and the characters. And yet its most impressive moment appears when it is not moving—the 14 minute rape scene. The contrast of stillness, the contrast of frozen observation, the continuous exploration of spaces, these recall Murnau, Freund, and Mayer—a camera played like a melody in movement.

TOUCH

Action cameras, like other wearable cameras, are carried on our bodies. They are attachments, and as attachments, they are still separated from our bodies but move with our bodies and their extensions. In a cyberpunk and cyborg phantasy of a human body, or a post-human body, the camera would be an implant in our bodies or a part of the body. Iraqi-born artist and New York University professor Wafaa Bilal mounted a camera to the back of his head in December 2010 for an art project. Why would somebody do something like this? Of course, sometimes we all wish to see what is behind us, to have a third eye.

»I am nothing if not a storyteller. My work to date has been concerned with the communication of public and private information to an audience so that it may be retold, distributed. The stories I tell are political dramas, which unfold through my past experience and into the present where they interact with the currency of media as the dialectic of aesthetic pleasure and pain.... During my journey from Iraq to Saudi Arabia, on to Kuwait and then the U.S., I left many people and places behind. The images I have of this journey are inevitably ephemeral, held as they are in my own memory. Many times while I was in transit and chaos the images failed to fully register, I did not have the time to absorb them. Now, in hindsight, I wish I could have recorded these images so that I could look back on them, to have them serve as a reminder and record of all the places I was forced to leave behind and may never see again.« (Bilal 2011)

The camera was attached with a magnetic camera mount. After doctors had refused to do the surgery, Bilal had the procedure done at a body-piercing studio in Los Angeles. The project, called *The 3rd I*, was created for an exhibition at the Arab Museum of Modern Art *Mathaf* in Qatar. The camera was mounted on a base inserted between Bilal's skin and skull (BBC News 2011).

On the his project website Bilal writes:

»The 3rdi arises from a need to objectively capture my past as it slips behind me from a non-confrontational point of view. It is anti-photography, decoded, and will capture images that are denoted rather than connoted, a technological-biological image. This will be accomplished by the complete removal of my hand and eye from the photographic process, circumventing the traditional conventions of traditional photography or a disruption in the photographic program. Barthes has said, '...from an aesthetic point of view the denoted image can appear as a kind of Edenic state of the image; cleared utopianically of its connotations, the image would become radically objective, or, in the last analysis, innocent.' It is this 'innocent' image that I wish to capture through the 3rdi.« (Bilal 2011)

In February 2011 the camera had to be removed as it posed a risk of infection for the artist.

Bilal's projects are often controversial. His 2008 work *Virtual Jihadi* was a video game in which an avatar of Bilal was a suicide bomber attempting to kill U.S. president George W. Bush (Ilnitzky 2011).

Of course, the implanted camera is a substantial element of body modifications in cyberpunk literature, films, and graphics. The implanted camera is superior to human eyes. The post-human creates a superior body. Bilal is not emphasizing the post-human; rather, he emphasizes the curiosity for looking at what is left behind our body. He extends the field of sight with his minute-by-minute snapshots, technically staying in the tradition and reality of photography and referring to it as a memory device. Unlike the works of the artist Stelarc, Bilal does not attempt to render the body obsolete (Stelarc 2014). The body is still a construct; the camera, even implanted, is an exterior object.

In 2012, a new fad swept Japan: a body art craze where people inject saline into their foreheads until a large welt forms. The bagel heads, as they are called, extend and modify the body's form beyond tattoos and piercings.

»It almost feels like something's dripping down my head. Is there something dripping down my head?" one man asks, as a thin tube pumps nearly 400 cc's of saline into his face. Some two hours later, after the gloved artist has pressed a gloved thumb into the swollen saline bubble, the man grabs mirror. 'I look delicious,' he quips. The procedure isn't permanent, and the bagel bump usually deflates in about a day as the body absorbs the saline,« (Bagel head 2012)

GLASSES AND WEARABLES

Wearable cameras similar to the implant camera automatically raise issues of privacy. While working at New York University, Bilal had to cover his head camera on campus. Google Glasses as well as wearable cameras, similar to the *Narrative Clip*, are always on and able to take single images in short intervals or even video; these create a feeling of constant surveillance, even in our intimate zones and personal areas. As we approach the idea of a recording person, we encounter different issues than being recorded by video surveillance in public or private spaces.

Early in 2014, the Internet was abuzz with the story of a man being removed from a cinema and interrogated for several hours because he was wearing a Google Glass; employees suspected that he was recording the film he was watching (AMC Theaters 2014).

Google Glass and the Narrative Clip camera are two different gadgets capable of being carried with us, but they operate in a similar context. The Narrative Clip is a simple camera shaped like a tie clip that takes a photo every 30 seconds. It can be clipped to anything we wear or carry. It is always on, unless you set it lens down or put it in the dark.

»Ostensibly you are supposed to wear it every day to record events (or non-events). It collects ambiance primarily. But it also just might capture that otherwise fleeting, single magic moment, which a regular camera could never get naturally. Leave it on all the time to shoot twice a minute, and the Narrative will record more than 2,800 images per day. The camera's 8GB of memory holds about 4,000 pictures total, so it's tough to fill it in a single day.« (Lasky 2014)

The camera is not yet video, but as ever-observant, wearable cameras become more popular and versatile, the step to video recording is not to far. The constant recording makes the camera invasive and creates another »Big Brother is watching« feeling. The Narrative Clip is still offline, whereas Google Glass is always connected to the Internet when in use. It only syncs to cloud servers when it is plugged in with its USB connection. It still has the character of a photographic diary, a more personal memory device, an innocent log.

»At the end of the day when you connect your Narrative to your computer's USB port, the thousands of pictures are uploaded to Narrative's servers and, if you want, backed up to your local hard drive. ... The rationale for the Narrative, much like competing devices from GoPro and Autographer, is to take those pictures that might have otherwise not been taken. The best result from my testing: I now have a flipbook of my friend's baby pugs frolicking, a capture of a moment that's not only priceless, but would otherwise not have been purposefully recorded. And the dogs didn't mind the camera always pointing at them. If the guys in the restaurant's men's room knew about it, I could have been in trouble. That's the thing about a wearable camera — you have to remember when to take it off.« (Lasky 2014)

It seems disturbing that the diary is on the manufacturer's cloud server and can be easily viewed on a smartphone. But why do people want to take a picture of their environment twice a minute anyway?

Nearly 3,000 people funded the Narrative Clip's Kickstarter campaign. Thousands are »lifelogging« with tools like FitBit. There must be a desire for a technology that is able to recall every single instant of our lives. There must be an obsession to not forget or to create a control mechanism to choose what to forget. Computers can track and store everything. They seem ideally suited to collect what appears scattered and unreliable, like our memories. But they do also more: »Yet even more than expanding my memories, I found my own camera companion was actually creating new ones« (Bosker 2014).

Wearable cameras move in the middle of our daily life. There is no longer differentiation between zones of privacy and public or business. These cameras will develop to come closer to our own skins and always on. There seems to be no escape. It is no longer a question of governing or control, but of habits and tastes. One day there will be a little ring on a finger with a little dot on it, and this object will be able to transmit an image or a sequence of images. People will wear little cameras as fetishes and memory devices; they will relive their rides as well as their intimate acts. As Jonathan Zittrain says: »People will put them on and wear them everywhere« (Eisenberg 2010).

Google Glass and the Narrative Clip are just the beginning new wearable technologies that sense the world around us. A layer of data, much like weather information, will overlay our own senses and we will experience rain not necessarily as a drop of water on our skin, but as information, as our wardrobe suggests that we wear something waterproof today. Wearable technology will create a barrier between the existing physical environment and us. The desire for wearable technology is generated through the need for this technology and its data.

»Data will not help you if you can't see it when you need it. For Dan Eisenhardt—a competitive swimmer for more than a decade, beginning as a 9-year-old in his native Denmark—the data he needed in the water, what he could never know in the water, was his splits. His event was the 1,500-meter freestyle, the longest slog in the sport, a near-mile of grinding exertion divided into 15 laps of 100 meters apiece. As with every distance sport, pacing is all; lag your target time on the first two laps and you may never catch up, but accidentally beat it and you'll load your tissue with lactic acid, doom your endgame. How fast was his last lap? How did it compare to his usual pace? His coach up on the pool deck could know, his parents in the stands could know. But Eisenhardt, at war in the water, could only guess.« (Wasik 2013)

TYRANNICAL LOOPS

Extended Vision—VINE

Twitter's mobile phone video app Vine allows users to record and post six-second video clips. Vine as a company was founded in June 2012 and bought by Twitter in October 2012. It debuted as a free IOS app on the iPhone and iPod Touch in January 2013 (Vine 2013).

Immediately after going public, it created a mass of hype and media coverage. Within a week, the first pornographic video clips appeared, and a Turkish journalist shared a video of the aftermath of a suicide bombing outside the U.S. embassy in Ankara, Turkey.

»The app records video as you hold your finger on the screen; removing the finger pauses the recording and allows you to make quick cuts to dissect your six seconds into one long shot, a couple short clips, or even many tiny brief shots to create stop-motion animation« (N. Jurgenson 2013b).

The impact of Vine was almost immediate. This was of course due to the ease of embedding the short videos on Twitter. Vine is not the first of its kind: debuting in 2010, Tout allows users to post 15-second spots.

Most of what is posted on Vine is simply of users doing things. The posts follow the usual Internet trends: users upload parodies of food eating, thousands and thousands of cat videos, and of course porn. Marketers and *wanna-be* independent moviemakers jumped on it.

What makes Vine interesting is that it places a rigid limit on the video, but also provides the ability to start and stop recording with a touch. Vine almost asks for a change of view, a creative usage or application. It stitches the world in three quick cuts together and therefore helps to document it differently.

»Vine is all to your advantage, it encompasses everything about what you do best. With Vine you can still devise clever plots, and awesome camera shots, use creative cuts, and compose thought-provoking juxtaposition that highlights your cinematography and directional skill. With your ability to mash it all in to six second clips even further demonstrates your superior talent as a filmmaker. Filmmakers, and/or stop motion lovers, Vine is for you.« (IndieReign 2013)

Bobby Miller, a young short filmmaker, started a Kickstarter campaign in 2013 to buy lenses for his iPhone, aiming to use his mobile device as his primary tool. He quoted Francis Ford Coppola on his Kickstarter page:

»to me, the great hope is that now these little 8mm video recorders and stuff have come out, and some… just people who normally wouldn't make movies are going to be making them. And you know, suddenly, one day some little fat girl in Ohio is going to be the new Mozart, you know, and make a beautiful film with her little father's camera recorder. And for once, the so-called professionalism about movies will be destroyed, forever. And it will really become an art form. That's my opinion.« (IndieReign 2013)

For Bobby, a revolution is at his fingertips. The formerly complex apparatus of filmmaking is readily available and creates an exciting future for new independent filmmaking.

»Vine feels pure. In six seconds, you have to convey something through a series of shots. And it's all done with 'in camera' editing. You don't have to ask permission to make them. And you can't monetize it. I think the last thing is pretty big, because it eliminates the need to satisfy anyone but yourself.« (IndieReign 2013)

The author of the blog post about Bobby sums it up: »We are in to an age where hand-held cameras, smart-phone/iPhone recordings have decent enough quality for the big screens and critics review these films, all looking for something 'raw' or 'real', which is so achievable now with small-budget films.« (IndieReign 2013)

The BBC News reports

»Six things people have learned about six-second video in a week:

1. Stop motion animation is alive and well
2. Ads work at six second length
3. People tend to do rather than say
4. Artificial limits help hype a social media offering
5. Aggregations of Vine are mesmerizing
6. Cats/porn dominate every platform on the internet.« (Roher 2013)

The limit of six seconds is received not as a narrative limitation but as a challenge. From a filmmaker's viewpoint, videos don't need to be feature length, and have never been. A story does not unfold in 90 minutes. These are industry standards. The short time we need to spend in transition needs shorter assemblages.

Stories for or from transition have a long oral tradition and are combined with any change of location. Stories of famous travelers like Marco Polo in the 13th century are common in our narrative repertoire.

The early days of cinema included numerous travelogues consisting of images from far away, places the industrial worker would never be able to travel that would come to entertain him through the cinematograph. Edison Motion Pictures in 1900 released several shots from Paris and the Swiss Alps. *Exotic Europe*, a DVD collection of early European travelogues following an exhibition from 2000, includes cheese making in Holland and the most beautiful waterfalls in the eastern Alps, the Turkish bazar in Sarajevo and Hungarian folklore.

Through commercials and television advertisements, narrative moving image forms with durations around 30 seconds to 1 minute have become standardized. Meanings are condensed and intensified. Their narrative function is to create the maximum impact on the audience, which means to gain full attention in a very short time period and maintain this attention. Good advertisements are those you might have talked about while waiting in transition or spending leisure time with friends. Successful commercials now are the ones that get shared and go viral. We talk about them on various social media outlets and link to them on the web. Narrative is just one possible element in the range of promotional tools. A range of genre classifications is at hand for the short form of the commercial spot.

The music video established another short form combining the traditions of the television commercial with experimental film and avant-garde practices to promote music visually. What led to the development of music television channels like MTV are films like the ones produced with the Beatles, which are not based on one consistent narrative; rather, they are interrupted, fragmented, and built around the band, the band members, and most importantly the songs. As early as the 1940s in the US, »jukebox films,« which were three-minute loops of musical promotional films, and Scopitone films were viewable on special viewing machines in bars and restaurants (Scopitone 2014).

In the late 2000s and towards the end of the DV-revolution, festivals, broadcasters, and cultural funding institutions came up with competitions and screenings of short forms like one-minute challenges around the world. Video technology had become affordable. MiniDV or digital video, in conjunction with editing and assembling software packages like Final Cut or Adobe Premiere, professionalized a wide range of wanna-be filmmakers.

The mobile phone industry quickly jumped on this bandwagon by integrating video on their mobile phones. Nokia held competitions for short fictional narrative forms produced with its mobile devices. The Nokia competitions and the marketing of its mobile phones created worldwide attention with its 15-second approach in 2003. Nokia teamed up with »British Independent Film Awards and Raindance Film Festival to encourage new film making talent and explore the links between mobile phones and film« (British Independent 2003).

»The introduction of video technology on mobile phones opens the door to a new and exciting medium for the viewing and production of film. Whether you're looking to take footage of family and friends or simply experiment with film, the opportunities offered by the combination of video and mobility are virtually endless.« (British Independent 2003)

The company aimed at young short filmmakers or young people dreaming of a possible career in the film industry. Together with festival organizers, schools, and professional organizations, they pushed to reanimate the short film as the path to stardom and build up new success stories from unknown talent around the world. The next step beyond the festivals was online sharing of the winning films, but the real purpose of this was to create a community for the brand through it.

Vine in one instant followed the same track. Bobby Miller's reference to Francis Ford Coppola summoned the tradition of cinema and placed the app in the moviemaking timeline. But Vine is used in many different ways. In Fall 2013 at a university in Izmir, hundreds of students gather to participate in an event called »Vine Phenomena« (Vine Fenomenleri 2013). Similar to a talk show with elements of standup comedy, the events invited several young Turkish Vine personalities to appear on stage; to the applause of their fans, they discussed their practices, repeated their jokes, and commented on daily situations, banalities, and political realities. The event became like a huge party for a couple of hours with newly born celebrities that many of the students hadn't heard of some time before, but had seen some of their clips and shared their jokes recently.

Cat porn and banalities seem to be most of what is shared throughout the *twitterverse* with Vine. The first trial of the app is usually recording anything the eye catches at that instant. Videos from offices, homes, schools, gardens, parties, and traffic are uploaded, including embarrassing incidents, the return of the animated gif, and dancing cats. Various aggregators like Vinepeek or Justvined assemble Vine videos. It is fascinating to watch the passing by of six-second slices of normal and ordinary lives.

The 2014 Tribeca Film Festival Vine contest winners were a stop-motion piece that turns a wrap into a break-dancer and a girl's drama of addiction. In the comedy category, a writer with a gorilla's head rises to fame after a falling cup serves as the traumatic inspiration to write a story. The audience award went to a pepper-shaker-stop-motion short called »Shaking Free,« in which a shaker falls on its side and the peppers falling create a human who then runs away. As the website confirms, the festival makers noted an increase in the quality of the Vine submissions.

»At last year's TFF, Vine was brand new and many creators were just beginning to get their hands dirty.... A year later, there is more mastery of the platform and the increased creativity and quality of stories is apparent« (Diaz 2014).

Tyrannical Loops

Whitney Erin Boesel, a Boston resident and sociology grad student, blogged about Vine footage taken during the Boston Marathon bombings.

The six-second loop captures the moment of the first bomb's explosion; that instant in which the atmosphere at this well-attended, annual public event was shattered (Baraniuk 2013). »In shooting a [V]ine of the explosion footage, the person who did so created an easily sharable short story of this afternoon's events that reduces the tragedy of a violent act down to a bright orange flash« (Boesel 2013).

I have not yet discussed one of the main elements of the Vine experience—the loop. The six-second video loops endlessly till I stop it. When my finger touches the screen, it stops playing. Vine loops like an animated GIF.

»If Wes Anderson was Instagram before Instagram, Miranda July Pinterest before Pinterest, Vine feels like a Darren Aronofsky montage: Dog sushi computer baby bowling guy beer concert train cooking kid cat shot-glass sports video game eating fireplace cab-ride thinking about what comes next feels a bit addictive.« (N. Jurgenson 2013b)

Nathan Jurgenson relates the Vine experience to Darren Aronofsky's editing style: our daily experiences are reflected in new forms of experience in today's actual cinema. Vine for Jurgenson trains us to see the world as it is quickly stitched together. As Stephen Shapiro pointed out in his discussion of post-cinematic affect, because our experiences break with continuity and are seduced by feelings, in the post-cinema the distinction between event and representation no longer exists. The world of the Internet and applications like Vine are not separated from the real world. What was once seen as bordered and framed is now penetrated and merged with no real difference. We are surrounded by moving images and we depend on them for our real interactions. The limit (or freedom) of Vine provides us with the ability to act in this way.

»What strikes me most about Vine and Vinepeek is the visual efficiency at play. It's what keeps me watching. In all honesty, the individual Vine, like a random photograph on Facebook, is pretty boring. As things go, the novelty outdoes the quality. But the trivial nature of most of the individual Vines becomes fascinating in aggregate. It might be the very triviality that seems profound: that so much minutia from across the globe comes together so instantly just for us on our screens. The individual Vine, with its short time-limit and quick cuts, encourages the creator to pack in lots of information in minimal time, a quantity exaggerated by Vinepeek playing them one-after-another. The dullness of the images intensifies this effect, shifting the focus from quality onto the spectacle of quantity.« (N. Jurgenson 2013b)

Intensification is the keyword to what is happening with clips, single shared videos. Cinema in past years already used methods of what David Bordwell calls intensified continuity, primarily in action movies. Now intensified continuity is a dominant style in popular mass cinema.

Following Bordwell, »intensified continuity is traditional continuity amped up, raised to a higher pitch of emphasis.« He identifies four tactics of camerawork and editing as characteristics: rapid editing, bipolar extremes of lens lengths, closer framing in dialogue scenes, and a free-ranging camera (Bordwell 2002).

Intensified continuity goes back to the demands of television: smaller screens needed closer shots. Video on mobile phones already automatically engages the viewer with closer action and more details than landscapes. The video recording device in the observer's hand is shaky; it concentrates on aspects of the moment, and might switch between recordings with change in positioning of the observer/recordist.

»Vine being what it is, this visual short story also does its own work to rapidly become the image of these events that its viewers have seen the greatest number of times (no broadcast network sensationalism required). One might argue that this self-repeating aspect makes Vine a powerful tool for reporting, but just because Vine can be used this way doesn't mean it should be used this way. And Vine definitely shouldn't be used this way without careful reflection about what it means to put six violent seconds on infinite (and infinitely circulative) self-repeat.« (Boesel 2013)

An incident depicted with Vine loops over and over. It is fixed, stocked with the dominating image. The image of the explosion becomes a perceived reality, discontinued from the real without explanatory continuity. As an artifact reminding us of the zoetrope and the animated GIF, it causes disturbance.

The Boston bombing looped reminds us of the news media coverage of the September 11, 2001 attacks on New York and Washington, DC (known forever in shorthand as 9/11). Scott Blake's artwork the *9/11 Flipbook* points toward »this endless repetition of the moment of destruction enabled perpetuation of that destruction, not simply its documentation« (Baraniuk 2013). Is the reply a good thing?

Among the first journalistic uses of Vine was, as I mentioned, a video of the aftermath of a suicide-bombing at the U.S. Embassy in Ankara in early 2013. Television audiences are used to repetitive loops of catastrophic events in daily news broadcasts all over the world. Through repetition, the violent image lacks substance; or, let's say that without its original narrative or factual context, it is infinitively decontextualized as an expression or a gesture of an affect.

Jean Baudrillard wrote in his essay *The Violence of the Image*, »The image [...] is violent because what happens there is the murder of the Real.... Particularly in the case of all professional or press-images which testify of real events. In making reality, even the most violent, emerge to the visible, it makes the real substance disappear« (Baraniuk 2013).

Chris Baraniuk, in discussing the effect on the viewer of looping violent images, also points to Douglas Rushkoff's latest book *Present Shock*, which describes the phenomenon and its effects as endemic. Like chickenpox, looping images are an infection maintained without any need for external input. They spread automatically.

»In the 1990s and 2000s, TV writers responded to dwindling and apathetic audiences by eradicating narrative complexity from story lines and prioritizing the spectacle-punctuated format of "reality" television« (Baraniuk 2013).

The impact of repeated exposure to media images of traumatic events is spoken of a great deal on the Internet, but it is also more serious. According to research published in the journal *Psychological Science,* it is potentially harmful to mental and physical health. Repeated exposure can correlate with incidences of acute stress (Association for Psychological Science 2012).

»As the moment of the spectacle, the explosion, the gunshot, the knife entering flesh, becomes available, its transition from censorship to virulent image (in Baurdrillard's terms) seems instant. There is no middle-ground. The looped, six-second footage of an explosion in Boston becomes totalising and yet represents the implosion of everything that happened yesterday down to a single shareable token. It encapsulates the reductionism practised and perfected by news media and it allows the tyranny of the loop to suggest trauma which is, in fact, unending.« (Baraniuk 2013)

Jean Baudrillard calls these »spectacle of banality.« This banality under the circumstances of the Boston or Ankara bombing is our real pornography and our true obscenity. We are following our naive impulse of comforting ourselves in nothingness, of hiding and not wanting to be seen. The opposite would a shift to delirious exhibitionism, making ourselves visible at any price. We are bound in this situation of not wanting to be seen and being continuously visible. So, we are always being read and are easily readable. We have become images. As such, we easily give other images of feelings and desires without having any secrets left to lose. For Baudrillard, this is the deepest violence—violence against the individual. Furthermore, because it loses its symbolic origin, it becomes a violation of language in the operation of visibility, producing another image (Baudrillard n.d.).

The loop of the Vine video does not make us forget, but repeats the instance, the moving image over and over and therefore creates an act of violation on significance and the symbolic. It itself is a look as well as an affect. But Baudrillard also calls attention to the fact that violence done through the image is balanced by violence done to the image. Violence to the image is its exploitation as a pure document, a proof, as in the loop of the Boston bombing explosion. As Baudrillard writes, the image is killed by an overdose of meaning. Here we are no longer much different than the Byzantine Iconoclasts. It is a sign of our »ultimate morality and our total obscenity.« »In order for the meaning, for the message to affect us, the image has to exist on its own, to impose its original language.… Obscene is all what is unnecessarily visible, without desire and without effect. All what usurps the so rare and so precious space of appearances« (Baudrillard n.d.).

There is still the response of a vast majority of images, Vines, or Instagrams of funny things, which pretend to build an antithesis. These images are not online selves; they seem to be public selves, selves who have agreed to share with only the few they think are watching. Video in Vine is still rough. It is as rough as its users not pretending to create perfect images. The spectacular still needs to be constructed, filtered, edited, and smoothed. Instagram—primarily an image-sharing service and secondarily with its 15-second videos following the Vine hype—is more about crafting visual phantasies, producing alternative visions of ourselves, more beautiful memorabilia (Wortham 2013).

Personally shared online video might already be becoming more intimate. The acquisition of Whatsapp by Facebook in 2014 points to such a direction. Whatsapp appears to be more intended for direct strong contacts and relations, while in its deep structure it seems more obvious and easy to be watched, pointed out, and followed.

Vine is naively just one possibility of personal documentation available for the online connected user. A tweet, a Facebook status, or a photograph shared on Flickr or Instagram are other possibilities to transmit a personal document, a share of privateness or public interest as well as a public activity. Photos, video, text, and audio are used in variations and combined in multiple and different forms for various audiences.

A Vine could be simply a life seen and documented for six seconds—a document, a vision, and a phantasy that produces a new kind of audiovisual literacy refurbishing and making public what was or is documentary and documentation.

Repeat!

Vine seems to be the rebirth of early cinema in the hand of a smartphone-owner. The history of the moving image already follows a history of centuries of visual loops and techniques of image repetition. Early cinema, born with the sneezing of Edison's assistant, reproduces the loop to install its very first commercial outlets. The nickelodeon enters the world out of the possibility of looping visual events with filmstrips.

The thaumatrope, daedelum (»the wheels of death«), and the zoetrope (»the wheels of life«) of the Victorian period were the realization of the idea of a visual loop.

»Shadow puppets, marionettes, automatons—all have long histories in both Western and Eastern culture, but the magic of the zoetrope was its perpetuity. Start the zoetrope spinning and suddenly a collection of static pictures begins an endless and mesmerizing dance.
The zoetrope effect presents a kind of paradox. Something, some action, is fixed for us within the confines of the loop. It is divorced from the linear nature of reality in this way. However, the zoetrope also brings "dead" frames of an animation to life, pulling static imagery together into an illusion of something composite and real.« (Baraniuk 2013b)

There are also Edward Muybridge's movement studies, which were designed to be played back over and over. Early film is from a scientific perspective a study of movement. The loop documents the rhythm of the movement of an object, its length (assuming real-time playback) the speed of the movement Each single frame proofs the objects moving parts position in a frozen still, the change in location and appearance. A change in appearance is the result of a movement. The loop makes this understandable and infinite.

In 2001, Lev Manovich discussed in his *The Language of New Media* the loop as narrative engine.

»Cinema's birth from a loop form was reenacted at least once during its history. In one of the sequences of *A Man with a Movie Camera*, Vertov shows us a cameraman standing in the back of a moving automobile. As he is being carried forward by an automobile, he cranks the handle of his camera. A loop, a repetition, created by the circular movement of the handle, gives birth to a progression of events—a very basic narrative which is also quintessentially modern: a camera moving through space recording whatever is in its way. In what seems to be a reference to cinema's primal scene, these shots are intercut with the shots of a moving train. Vertov even re-stages the terror which Lumieres's film supposedly provoked in its audience; he positions his camera right along the train track so the train runs over our point of view a number of times, crushing us again and again.« (Manovich 2001)

It was Méliès' fascination with movement that brought him to cinema, prompting the desire for fascinating journeys, more and more, over and over. In one of his first enterprises as a new filmmaker, Méliès traveled several times from Paris to the coast and back to get a single strip of film exposure—the tidal wave I mentioned earlier, which would create the marvelous, astonishing impression of the power of nature equal to the power of moving things. In this sense, the movies are simply born out of things moving.

And our fascination with movement gave birth to another ancestor of Vine as well—the GIF. The GIF translates into the Internet and still exists as fresh as it was when the file format was developed and presented in 1987. The CompuServe 87a's graphic interchange format was created to add moving imagery to static web pages without the necessity of high bandwidth; it was also designed to be portable and compatible between browsers. The GIF format supports 8 bits of information per pixel and was therefore very suitable for light, brief animations with small file sizes. The format is now back to life in microblogging sites like Tumblr as well as in social media outlets like Facebook. It is no longer simply a moving decoration or element begging for attention; rather, it has become an element of communication and exchange. The format is used for looped gestures and comments between users in place of emoticons. Fragments of fiction films and Hollywood movies duplicate looped human gestures and responses in dialogue settings (GIFGIF 2014).[1] The looped GIF as visual response has become a gesture. Animated GIF's as memes are familiar elements of Internet remix culture. The loops gesture is more than simply the repetition of some still frames or the framework for animation of inanimate objects, it is funny, absurd, critical, brutal, cruel, and/or embarrassing in repeating a captured momentum ad infinitum.

In *Notes on Gesture*, the last chapter of *History & Infancy*, Georgio Agamben tells of an interesting symptom recorded by physicians at the end of the 19th century: the loss of gestures among urban (bourgeois) people, people forgetting the manners of walking or having disorders (such as uncontrollable jerking) while doing simple everyday gestures (Agamben 2006). Agamben writes that with the start of the 20th century, this issue was no longer noticed—not only because this state became »normal,« but mainly because a »machinery of gestures« arose. Following Deleuze, Agamben describes cinema as producing gestures—blocks of space and movement, which are basically gestures. Thus, a new kind of production of gestures replaced the loss of gestures. The state Agamben describes before the turn of the 19th century is a state of alienation, a response of the body when it suddenly falls into another form of life. The stranger forgets how to walk, how to move his hands, how to point, and how to look. This state is overcome with the help of the cinematic machinery.

---

[1] »An animated gif is a magical thing. It contains the power to convey emotion, empathy, and context in a subtle way that text or emoticons simply can't. GIFGIF is a project to capture that magic with quantitative methods. Our goal is to create a tool that lets people explore the world of gifs by the emotions they evoke, rather than by manually entered tags. « (GIFGIF 2014).

In his blog post *The Wheel of the Devil*, Chris Baraniuk writes »the reign of the loop is greatly empowered by digital media, and ... today loops have enriched culture while offering new perspectives on the nature of reality« (Baraniuk 2013b).

Artists have started to explore the low-resolution identity of the GIF and its looping function anew. Glitch art and found footage digitized clips are an oft-used material. Max Capacity creates gifs out of digitized clips of VHS video recordings. He states, »What these film loops offer is a mental state rather than a series of events. They convey a meditative, almost somnambulist, form of pleasure: nothing really happens, yet it's hard to stop watching« (Birnbaum 1999).

Some of Peter Land's ideas for his video works develop from the influence of slapstick silent films. In an interview, he recalls a massive pie fight at the end of one of Laurel & Hardy's films. »And I started thinking... what if the entire film would had only been about people throwing cakes into each other's faces? What about 100 scenes only with that, would it stay funny or would it turn into something else?« (Burugorri 2014).

One of his primary aims in his work is to use repetitive actions till they appear absurd and meaningless, as in the Theatre of the Absurd, where human existence has no specific purpose.

»I'm something quite different, a quite different thing, a wordless thing in an empty space, a hard shut dry cold black place, where nothing stirs, nothing speaks, and that I listen, and that I seek, like a caged beast born of caged beasts born of caged beasts born in a cage and dead in a cage, born and then dead, born in a cage and then dead in a cage, in a word like a beast.«[2]

The loop repeats and presents a new object, an action becoming absurd, losing its purpose and becoming meaningless, representing a constant failure, a struggle in an endless circle of repetition. Anything can become a GIF, anything can be looped to the point of absolute banality.

»The loop has the power to trap you, to absorb you, to get into your mind and don't let you stop watching it, to manipulate its meaning until it ends with it. Its hypnotic

---

2 Samuel Beckett. *The Unnamable* (1965), quoted in Birnbaum (1999).

appearance makes you enter in a sort of meditation state with which we inexplicably empathize.... It becomes about this very human condition of existence...it's also very much about the loss of control, this feeling that you are not the master of yourself anymore, something from the outside is somehow interfering with you, not in the psychotic way, but more like in a social way that makes it impossible for you to feel that you are directing your own actions.« (Burugorri 2014)

Illustration 3: Erdal İnci. Camondo Stairs.

Source: http://erdalinci.tumblr.com/ [2013]

Erdal Inci's *Patterns of Motion* uses Istiklal Avenue, Taksim Square, Galata Tower, and Camondo Stairs in Istanbul to serve as performance stages for his video loops. Inci depicts cycles of human movement at known touristic and historic places, creating living organisms by repeating their presence. On Camondo Stairs, hooded human clones descend in synchronized motion. Erdal does not only loop the motion; he multiplies it by cloning the moving object. At the same time, he references past events, not only the history of the stairs but also a photograph of Henri Cartier Bresson taken on these stairs in 1964. The loop of the clones is overloaded through location and object relations but at the same time by simple rhythm, a magic cycle, empty in eternal repetition. Inci clearly references principles of art making, the use of patterns, repetitions, motifs, and dance. His patterns of motion are set in the tradition of pattern in Turkish art, recalling the constellations of patterns in painting and dance.

For Chris Baraniuk, it is the hypnosis of the loop, the absence of a beginning and ending that makes it seem uncanny.

»Nonsensical yet enthralling, the loop of zoetrope or gif is like a broken record in that it captures a moment in which time has been made to maniacally repeat itself. This narrative dissonance, this psychotic imagery which implicitly begs to be halted or somehow set free is at odds with all other un-looped media.« (Baraniuk 2013b)

As I mentioned, Vine's six seconds might be a single shot or many shots cut together. It's easy to pause recording to change position or subject, and if you are unhappy with the recording, you simply start it over instead of uploading it.

After the recording is uploaded, the Vine video will appear looping. Baraniuk asks, why was the feature of the loop included? As he suggests, did the creators of Vine wanted to capitalize on the popularity of the animated GIF (Baraniuk 2013b)?

The loop function was present quite early in online video; it was a main element of the interface design and usage. Quicktime movies were supposed to be played forward, backward, and looped. Computer games heavily relied on the loop as well because of storage limitations. Characters, their movements, and their actions were designed in small loops and then recalled from the library when needed during game play. The use of loops declined with higher processor speeds and larger storage.

Lev Manovich emphasized in *The Language of New Media* that the loop not only gave birth to cinema but also is an essential element of programming (Manovich 2001). In the written structures of programs, clauses like »if/then« and »repeat/while« alter the linear flow of data. Most elementary of these control structures is the loop. It consists of a sequence of instructions that will be continuously repeated until the conditions are changed. Such a sequence could ask for a certain data input, such as a certain number. If this number is reached, the looping process stops and initiates a change, practically jumping to another string of instructions. An application or a program can be built on a series of loops analyzing and comparing data and defining a behavior of an object visible or invisible, temporary or permanent.

The loop is also the traditional tool and technique of classic cell animation. While the loop applies in general to everything that is displayed at once, a single object's movement is built by cycles for ease of reuse. For example, for a simple »run cycle,« in which a character's steps loop to create the illusion of running, the animator might have created only two different phases of the movement.

Sometimes a few looped frames are enough to produce the illusion of life and linear time. Sometimes even a small area in the visual field is enough to give the illusion of continued life. The application Echograph let users select a single frame from a video and then paint in an area where the video should be kept. The resulting clip is then created as a single frame with a looping movement part in it. A simple example could be a fire in an oven where only the flames are moving.

The Echograph blog from April 21, 2014 features a cat moving her head while the rest of the image and her body are blurred. A recent staff-picks newsletter features the Czech Republic Echographer, Dušan Vondra, and his Echograph animated photo series. One of his photographs features a group of musicians and a dancing woman on the streets. Only the drummer is moving, playing the drums while the others are frozen in the snapshot. The Echograph depicts two different times, a frozen still time, and a lively continuing time. Both single out a single object or event, a single change, while everything else is stopped.

Practically speaking, the user captures or imports a video into the application, trims the length down to five seconds or less, selects a still frame, decides in which area the movement should appear, and paints or brushes a mask. The operation of painting on a video to mask a part of its content is already used in programs like Adobe After Effects or the Avid Media Composer (Magic Mask), programs used by professional media creators.

In addition, it is also possible to reverse the direction of the video, which the creators call »palindroming«: the meaning stays the same forward and backward while adding a delay to make the final experience smoother. As the application is designed for tablets and smartphones, all these functions appear at the lower corners of the screen. For the backdrop the tutorial suggests choosing an aspect of motion of the main subject to be frozen in the frame (Echograph n.d.). The app itself guides the user through the process while using standard interactive design conventions to keep the process simple.

Echographs are called visual stories by their developers as each operates at least of two levels of narration, with the frozen backdrop setting the scene and the moving video element as a second level, detail, or character. The narrative relation is constructed inside the frame, similar to graphical literature and comics.

Artists Jamie Beck and Kevin Burg explored a similar process and effect in the GIF format around 2009. They called their style the *Cinemagraph*: »A Cinemagraph is an image that contains within itself a living moment that allows a glimpse of time to be experienced and preserved endlessly« (Cinemagraphs n.d.).

In the process, the artists take a traditional photograph and place a living moment into the image through the isolated animation of multiple frames. After launching their work mainly through Twitter and Tumblr, their style of imagery and its name became a new GIF genre. The strength of cinemagraphs is the illusion of watching a video, but in reality it is just an animated GIF with sequential frames embedded. What's the difference between this and simple animated text, emoticons, funny scenes, and cats' tails? As Joshua Cohen pointed out, cinemagraphs consist of beautiful images with touches of continuous movement, and are therefore also a genre of animated GIFs for adults (Cohen 2011).

Beck explained how cinemagraphs helped him see the world differently. »I was shooting a building to make a cinemagraph one day, and nothing moved. I thought, well this is dumb.... But then the light changed, a bird flew by, and I realized that everything is alive. I just had to start training my eye. I had to start visualizing cinemagraphs« (Desertmoondubai 2012). Burg agrees. »I'm forced to learn new things every time I create a cinemagraph. I learn how to better control things, and how to better explain what's happening in the picture« (Flock 2011).

Beck and Burg come from fashion photography and are emphasizing a certain aesthetic appearance combined with appealing movements and visual surprises. They emphasize visual style and appeal. Cinemagraphs not only appear to be the grown-up form of the GIF and GIF animation, they must be seen in the context of a visual literacy that has already experienced bullet time, the DSLR revolution, and the collapse of video making and photography into a single device. They are an element of a visual language that depicts an internal reality embedding a multiplicity of time. The cinemagraph as well as its follower, the echograph, contrasts linear present time flow with frozen past time, creating an image that before now has been science fiction.

GENERATIO AEQUIVOCA

The digital loop reflects back on filmmakers and influences their work in the framework of the white cube as cinema and television are no longer primary facilitators. Filmmakers cross over to the visual arts. Dan Oki is a Croatian filmmaker and visual artist whose work crosses the borders between classic cinema and the visual arts without explicitly relating to video art. Oki brings together principles and concepts from experimental film, databases, video, animation, web, photography, and performance. His 2008 work *Generatio Aequivoca* shows in a single looped clip a variety of playful young swimmers in the water at a beach close to Split in Croatia.

Illustration 4: Dan Oki. Generatio Aequivoca.

Source: kipla.org

The frame does not include a horizon. The shot is taken from a distance with a telephoto lens, bringing objects and people in the water closer together and filling the frame with the swimmers. The telephoto lens effect flattens the image as it collapses the depicted space. Oki's image recalls Pieter Bruegel's 1560 painting *Children's Games*. Like Bruegel, Oki shows the children and adults seriously absorbed in their games. The loop of the video emphasizes the play and continues its life on the screen. The amount of repeating movement in the image keeps the attention of the viewer away from a simple rhythmic pleasure and makes invisible the technical characteristics of repetition and the cycle of the loop.

»Generatio Aequivoca (2008) is based on one of the most important theses of evolutionary theory, according to which 'spontaneous generation' is a proof of continuous evolution of the organic, a proof that living beings are not static, but constantly evolving, and that living organisms developed from inanimate matter. By doing so, it dismisses creationist theories and the belief in the existence of the divine, placing on the pedestal the mighty nature in all its complexity. Generatio Aequivoca reflects the world view of Dan Oki, who uses his work to praise nature and celebrate life with a positive attitude. The 'spontaneous generation' thesis was chosen as a framework for a poetic story about the future generation, which will decide the fate of the world based on its own aspirations, experience and values, partly inherited from its ancestors.« (Colner 2011)

Oki's sensibility lays open the fragility and magnificence of life in the observation of life. What was once embedded in the »wheel of death« is projected through a modern method that lets the video appear to be almost lifelike, capturing the pleasure of childish play.

ENTER FRAME

Digital video itself points to the idea of the loop as an engine. As I mentioned, early Quicktime videos included looping functions. Here, the loop's main purpose was to play the video again and again as an extension of the viewing experience. The videos were short because of storage and bandwidth restrictions. It's also possible that the loop was included because it was easy to include it, since there was no longer any need to rewind videos. In the early stages of the web, the video loop function was not necessarily related to the use of video as a way of producing the illusion of a living object in a digital environment. Games like *Myst* and its sequel *Riven* used short sequences of looped frames as major elements in the players' on-screen experience. The loop was used as the narrative engine of the game.

Within (and with) the loop, video and animation merge. Both use the same single unit; a video clip and an animation are based on the frame as complex carrier of dynamic information. Cinemagraphs and Vines are basically different, but they are similar in their playback functions. Both appear linear, but one is based on animated frames, whereas the other is based on recorded frames.

If the clip would be my single LEGO stone, then the frame would be its size. As multimedia authoring has taught through programs like Macromedia Director or Flash, a movie and therefore a complex interactive experience can consist of a single frame in the score of the event, but it can also consist of an endless series of frames following and played in sequence. The program writes a stop and creates a loop on a single frame, or perhaps on a frame after a linear sequence of multiple frames leading towards the stop; it could demand input or change through an action from outside of the frame. What makes a video and what makes a clip is the completeness of the information created at once in a single frame and its linear continuation in time. The cinemagraph becomes a video only if it would be projected as such. The GIF animation becomes more video-like if it appears under the same conditions in its projection or presentation.

John Cage suggested the frame as a basic unit to measure time in his 1937 essay "The Future of Music" (Cage 1937). Thinking of the frame as a basic unit for time means to think in clearly defined fractions, but also to adopt the idea of cinema and the principles of film technique. In the context of Cage as a composer of avant-garde music it means to describe or create music with or through a cinematic system:

»Cage was already prepared to think in terms of music as cinematic apparatus composed via a system driven by external events and not prescriptions. Cage was prepared to accommodate accident within structure, and was not afraid of electronic instruments. If we switch the phrase 'composer of sound' for 'author of media' we find ourselves in some version of Cage's predicted frame-driven future. From megahertz to refresh rates, the computing environment is a choreography of events possessing the complexity and precision of a Balinese gamelan, operating at speeds that border on the unimaginable. Digital representations require the definition of discrete steps, and cannot avoid being reduced to absolute minutiae, like sprockets along the edge of film. The majority of time-based authoring tools use the metaphor of the frame, and are able to operate at increasingly flexible tempos that can take us from time-lapse to bullet-time.« (Goldberg 2002)

What Cage couldn't know when he wrote the text was that the frame itself could become a flexible unit, losing its geometrical and its sequential mechanical conditions. A single frame today is actually extended beyond its physical appearance, carrying layers of connections and relations, embedding complete entities, objects, or sequences; and it can be aware of its own content as well as its environment. In some ways, it is a state of all conditions associated with it. While before a frame was a part of a sequence and therefore had a distinct duration, now the frame itself determines duration and space. What is digital video is defined as an element that obeys its frame rate while itself being the superior meaningful structure.

INFINITY

Is this flood of looped short instances of moving images another wish to overcome death, to extend life endlessly? Is the looping of video another attempt to capture us and hold our souls in prison? Or is it just the need to keep the channel of transmission open so that certain images can reach us? The looping jump of a cat is by no means something worth remembering. What matters is the recorded and repeated movement, the difference between two images or two frames. Movement overcomes the rigidity of the frame and leaves the single image. Movement embeds infinity, longing beyond the imaginable.

Gilles Deleuze has already predicted what is suggested in his description of two planes—the image and the infinite. These two planes constantly unfold and enfold. They form the boundary between the virtual and the actual. Experience, information, and the image are set in relation to each other. To look at a clip looping infinitely and at a clip of a single frame's duration recalls the condition of the brick with its necessary dimensions that allow it to fit in context or to be combined with other bricks.

Length or duration is one unit. The other essential unit is the timeline or the time string.

Duration

How long does a clip last? The length of the clip is defined by the number of frames that make it up. Cinema has a worldwide standard of 24 frames per second. Video in Europe plays at 25 frames per second, whereas on U.S. television it's almost 30 frames per second (29.97, to be exact). A clip of a single frame is just a single frame presentation in a timeline; without a loop, it takes just a tiny instant of time. Duration is measured not only in clear units but also in subjective experience. The experience of a flow of images in a clip—a movement, an action, something we're looking at—can feel subjectively like different durations to different observers. The perception of time of the clip can be influenced or manipulated through the sequence of events the clip belongs to as well as by the elements embedded in the clip, their formal composition, and the emotions the clip provokes. Even if the duration is constant, time can be compressed or stretched.

WAYS OF SEEING

> "I must begin, not with hypothesis, but with specific instances, no matter how minute."
>
> PAUL KLEE

MAGIC

The web is full of clips that express the fascination we have with time and movement. Every day new sensational or unusual time-lapses and slow-motions are uploaded somewhere, to be discovered and shared. On April 22, 2014 the photography-related site PetaPixel promoted *Slow Motion Aerial Video Takes You Inside a Fireworks Show*:

»Slow-motion footage is cool. Camera copter footage is cool. Fireworks are cool. So what happens when you mash all of them together into one video? No worries, your head won't explode (mostly because the GoPro this was probably filmed on doesn't do so hot in super low light) but the resulting video is a mesmerizing two and a half minute experience. « (Cade 2014)

To produce slow motion, footage is recorded at a rate of up to several hundreds of frames per second; a time-lapse is the opposite, with perhaps only one frame captured in a distinctive time interval. One typical time-lapse video that went viral was Christoph Rehage's *The Longest Way 1.0 - walk through China and grow a beard* (Rehage 2009). In 2008, Rehage walked more than 4500 km through China for a year. In March 2009, he uploaded a video consisting of still shots from different locations showing him centered in the frame, revealing his beard and hair growing out.

Rehage's video belongs to a range of time-lapse videos documenting personal change in style, appearance, or growth, but it also includes change in location. Single frames can be recorded several minutes or hours or days apart; distances can change from meters to thousands of kilometers. Of course, after this practice went viral media institutions and advertisers adopted these formats, so at some point in the web timeline of the last year it became impossible to tell whether such a video had been produced through the natural instinct of its creator (the self-depicting person or shooter) or by somebody with a commercial interest at heart.[1]

In recent years, time-lapses have been produced with cameras installed on supporting devices like sliders, mini-cranes, and remote-controlled camera heads. The supporting tools are connected to micro-controllers that interface with computers to time and orchestrate precise camera movements. Camera and supporting devices are programed to combine change in time with change in space. For example, the fast movement of clouds over New York's Times Square is combined with a horizontal camera movement dollying parallel to objects at street level.

The magic or visual trickery is not only fascinating but also becoming easier to produce with affordable everyday technology. Together with the rise of the maker movement in the U.S., the rise of do-it-yourself technology for supporting tools follows advances in camera development. Photography meets video meets physical computing. The DSLR revolution launched with Canon's 5D Mark II camera only a few years ago has already created a market for new companies building supporting rigs and cages to create stabilized camera movements; people with a do-it-yourself outlook can build their own sliders.

The camera manufacturers of the classic film industry are surrounded by a small industry that builds precise tools and gear to support camera attachment and rigging for simple to complex camera movements in space. These tools are adjusted to the need of n moving image producing industry

---

1 See BachiRules (2012), Bliss (2013), and Hofmeester (2013) for examples.

to produce precisely composed and directed results on demand surrounded by operating specialists.

Movement in the frame and movement with the camera are problematic and result in disturbing artifacts. Traditionally video cameras used CCD sensors, while newer cameras are using CMOS sensors. Both type of image sensors have their own unique properties and characteristics. CMOS sensors are more energy efficient and use less battery life. They transport and upload data faster. But they also produce skew, wobble and partial exposure, what CCD chips don't do (Green n.d.).

»Rolling shutter artifacts – the so-called 'jello-o-cam' effect – have been the bane of CMOS-sensor cameras, most notably the HD-capable DSLR still cameras. The short answer for why this happens is that objects move in place during the time interval between the data being picked up from the top to the bottom of the sensor. The visual manifestation is skewing or a wobble to the image on fast horizontal motion or shaky handheld shots.« (Salvia 2010)

Visual wobbling and video jelly are the side effects of the usage of photographic gear and cheap high resolution CMOS sensor technology and is compensated through expensive plug-ins for postproduction software tools like Final Cut Pro or Adobe After Effects. »To eliminate wobble you would need to either a) eliminate all motion, or b) use a global shutter system. Since neither of these are practical options for a video camera using a CMOS sensor, you will have to determine if the amount of wobbling that happens in video is acceptable to you« (Salvia 2010).

BOKEY-PORN

The DSLR revolution brought high-resolution video into the hands of photographers. The first excitement was not just the price and the high-quality film-like image, but also the use of narrow depths of field or shallow focus through various lens selections to create a blurred look in various parts of the image. This blur in the out-of-focus areas of an image is called Bokeh (or Bokey), from a Japanese word meaning blur or haze.

Florian Cramer, at the sixth annual Video Vortex conference in Amsterdam, pointed to what he called Bokeh porn: a wide range of DSLR videos demonstrating the new tools and their ability to shoot excellent videos in a range of situations while at some time the object of interest itself comes into the frame. The blur or bokeh is no longer an aesthetic quality of the image but has become the main aspect of the video.

»Let me ask you something. When was the last freakin' time you watched a film at the cinema when every shot, and I mean EVERY SHOT had extremely shallow depth of field? Never, that's when. In fact many 35mm filmmakers aim for DEEP depth of field« (Wyndham 2010). Simon Wyndham provocatively expresses what he is observing, namely that videos shared on sites like Vimeo tend to appear as test films—camera tests without any narrative approach that use shallow depth of field using the presets of Magic Bullet software filters. Without these tricks, the videos would be dull and lifeless.

»So instead we get test films. Over and over again. Want to make that film you've always dreamed of? You know, the one about picking your nasal hair from your nose? Well now you have a valid outlet. Get yourself a Canon 5D and everyone can now enjoy your crusty snot covered shallow depth of field nasal hair being pulled from its roots in glorious high definition to the sound of Pink Floyd's "Brick In The Wall".« (Wyndham 2010).

Of course, Florian Cramer is not following Simon Wyndall's blog rant; rather, he's pointing out what is becoming obvious in the DSLR and digital camera revolution: filmmaking becomes a demo. The process of production is central, instead of cinematographic experimentation, exploration of filmic language or style, or any narrative approach. The technology is the social connecting factor. The videos are followed by discussions and exchange of tips and tricks. Other videos connect in the same explanatory manner, socializing imaging technology. The camera reframed in the image of such videos even becomes an author. Following Cramer, bokeh creates a narrative that abstracts the process of filmmaking.

Early Vimeo-shared videos on gear like the Canon 5D or 7D or the Panasonic GH2 placed the technology in the foreground, similar to automotive testing TV programs like BBC's *Top Gear*. The videos are about what the gear can do or not, pushing technical parameters to the foreground, engaging in pixel dimensions to simulate imaging tools for mass audiences, all unrelated their purpose of image-making. The videos project expertise. Analog aesthetics and practices are recalled and remixed.

LOOKING AT—CLIPS AS FORM OF SEEING

»If cinema has already revealed that the world is a flow of images and this world of images is in a state of constant transformation, then video technology causes a further deterritorialisation of these flows. Video technology not only shows us the movement, the never-ending variation of images, but also the 'time-matter' from which the images are made (the electromagnetic waves). Video technology is a mechanical arrangement that establishes a relationship between a-significant flows (waves) and significant flows (the images). It is the first technical means of producing images that reflects the 'general decoding of the flows'.« (Lazzarato 2007)

Maurizio Lazzarato underlines what is clearly the difference between cinema and video in terms of its technology of image production. Film makes the still photograph run through transport. The basic generic element of cinema is the photograph. Montage is the temporal generic element. Following Nam June Paik, video is simply time. What we are looking at when we look at a video is time. The photogram is a time frozen and archived; the video image doesn't exist at once, but is a continuous movement of light, writing differences in time. The difference between the photographic image and the recorded video image is not only the totality of the image at once, since this does not exist in video; rather, it is the rewriting of a movement, its repetition as it goes point by point and line by line, analyzing and re-analyzing its value, the strength of its light, and its position. Here, analysis is more a method and a mode.

Looking at video is not looking at the reflection of a past inscription, something, that *has been*; it is looking at something that *is*. The movement is there; it condenses or stretches a time, a period, a day, a life. We are seeing time.

The practice of looking through clips as they are shared online has expanded our ways of seeing (to refer to John Berger's well-known book of that title). These video clips have an enormous variety; they show or reflect a wide range of means. Every day, we are trying to make sense of the world around us. Practices of recording, sharing, and appreciating video clips are part of the process of recognizing the world around us. Looking at this world is an active process. It is a quest for purpose and direction. The shared videos connect our experiences. What we have seen is becoming what we all see even if it would be impossible for us to look at, perhaps because of our physical position, but perhaps because of the absence of our body's presence or absence of attention.

In 2013, Australian researcher Adrian Miles started another kind of inquiry into the use of Vine as a daily documenting tool. She combined the videos with a simple website. »Every morning, well, nearly every morning, around about 7am, I film the ridge over the way using Vine on my phone. A small daily gesture, inscribing a particular sort of observational media trail. The intent is to do this for a year. The First Quarter is a web based observational video work that uses the first three months of clips« (Miles 2013).

The Vine videos in a row and as a list obviously present a simple documentation of what Adrian Miles has recorded using Vine and therefore has lived on the specific days of the recordings. The place we see, the weather, the light—it has all been like this. But when we replay the clips, they are actualizing themselves again. A nonlinear sequence creates a new experience and a new life. We are looking at a time, which promises its flow and fulfills this promise. The movements are real, because it is now moving and we are looking at it.

To look at something involves a process. This process is not just a mechanical process of image-making; it is a process of defining an image through the process. This process is formed technologically through software and hardware. Hardware is an image sensor extended and attachable to any kind of body, body accessory, or object in extension of the human body. Software is the coding of the light information of the sensor. The video clip itself is the complexity of creation of the hardware and the software in the production of the flow. This flow is as much signal as it is image, but it is not necessary photographic.

Time has an explicit standing as processed video already in its production creates an elastic string of time, a rubber band. Time can be stretched.

ELASTIC REALITY

During the Video Vortex conference in Yogyakarta, Indonesia I experienced an understanding of time, which my colleagues named »rubber time.« In a very Western and European sense, the Latin phrase *sine tempori* defines an event to have taken place at the exact announced time; if instead *cum tempori* is mentioned, the event could start with a delay of as much as 15 minutes. Rubber time simply means that the event would start at *some* time. There is no exact unit of measurement. People would gather for about an hour, and the event would be about to start. Rubber time resists the exact limitation of time and rather engages everyone in a flexible and transformable use of time as a definition of being at a place.

The precise time and the exact number of frames for video to be recorded and played back are no longer rigid and dogmatic. The little stopwatch introduced in the tools of video editors and their timelines redefines an understanding of time. The point in the graphic of the video clip in the editor on screen where the stopwatch is applied defines a change in signal and flow through a change of time. The time base stays as a rhythm-giving device for playback, but the clip's internal time has changed.

Time lapses, hyper-timelapses, and slow-motions express the readjustment of time and its rubber use, its stretchability. Time is elastic.

»He remembers those vanished years. As though looking through a dusty windowpane, the past is something he could see, but not touch. And everything he sees is blurred and indistinct.« This short quotation, from the closing of Wong Kar-Wai's 2000 film *In the Mood for Love*, was quoted in film critic Mike D'Angelo's review of another film by the same Hong Kong director, the 1994 film *Chungking Express* (D'Angelo 2013). The latter film leaves the audience slightly puzzled by its breathtaking, impressionistic shooting style, its blurred slow-motions, its lively graininess of its shots, its vivid and contrasting colors, its fast cuts and pans. As Roger Ebert noted in his review, Wong Kar-Wai seems to be more concerned with the materials the story of the film is made of than the story itself (Ebert 1996).

The plot of the film consists of two different stories told one after the other. Each story is about a Hong Kong policeman and his romance or love affair with a woman. The two stories connect only at a brief intersecting moment in between, but otherwise have no real connections.

Mike D'Angelo, in his article *How Wong Kar-Wai Turned 22 Seconds into an Eterninty*, relinks the stories in the way the characters are related to time. The first story shows a mourning and waiting policeman who was dumped by his girlfriend. The relationship is already over, but it expires slowly in the portrait of the character. The second story relates to a date in the future. As D'Angelo points out, Wong Kar-Wai's characters are not living in the present of the story or their life. They are looking forward or backward, to stories of new or old love.

For one shot in the film (the 22 seconds of D'Angelo's title), Wong Kar-Wai and his cinematographers Andrew Lau and Christopher Doyle find a very special way to visually include a temporal distortion. While in the second story, the policeman character drinks a cup of coffee and the girl Faye is watching him while people in front of them move in fast speed, like a time lapse. The shot shows two levels of time as foreground and background.

Technically, in film the effect can be achieved by undercranking— shooting at a very low frame rate, perhaps 4 or 6 frames per second—and then step-printing the film in the lab to bring the footage back to normal speed. The shots like in *Chungking Express* and other Wong Kar-Wai films in cooperation with Christopher Doyle look more blurred because of the longer shutter speeds of undercranking. Similar shots using this technique can be found in the 2000 film *Gladiator*'s early battle scenes as well as many other films and almost all music videos (Deakins 2008).

In the cinematographic style of Christopher Doyle, the blurring of light and color and the use of slow motion and slow shutter speed amplify the emotional intensity and create an isolated self-awareness. The surroundings pass while the character is stuck. The audience also loses track of the environment. It becomes anytime. The shot is more an expression of feeling and an explanation of reason. The experience needs to be felt.

»Both of these stories, about disconnections, loneliness and being alone in the vast city, are photographed in the style of a music video, crossed with a little Godard (signs, slogans, pop music) and some Cassavetes (improvised dialogue and situations). What happens to the character is not really the point; the movie is about their journeys, not their destinations. There is the possibility that they have all been driven to desperation, if not the edge of madness, by the artificial lives they lead, in which all authentic experience seems at one remove.« (Ebert 1996)

For Roger Ebert, Wong Kar-Wai plays with our perception of cinema. The film is a product of pop culture, more about citing film and giving pleasure through its style than a story about life.

The emphasis on style was also appropriated in the decision of the Criterion Collection to release *Chunking Express* as its first Blu-Ray in 2008. For the film writer Glenn Kenny, the release is as much a surprise as it is a revelation that will thrill cinephiles. »Film grain, a bedbug of certain high-def advocates, is spectacularly intact, as the top screen shot attests. Indeed, Chungking Express is one of those films that thoroughly vindicates something film preservationist Robert Harris once said to me: 'The grain is the picture'« (Kenny 2008).

PROCESSED TIME

Adam Magyar is a photographer concentrating on street photography. In his practice, he is not interested in magical moments where a whole story comes together in one photograph; rather, he is attracted by the rest, the uninteresting and ignored moments. To capture what is behind those other moments, he experiments with various technologies not necessarily developed for photography. He became especially interested in slit scan photography. »Slit scan imaging techniques are used to create static images of time-based phenomena. In traditional film photography, slit scan images are created by exposing film as it slides past a slit-shaped aperture. In the digital realm, thin slices are extracted from a sequence of video frames, and concatenated into a new image« (Magyar 2014).

Magyar talks about using industrial cameras and computers to photograph and process urban images that capture a moment of time and then visually expand it. He calls it the »transformation of reality by the camera« (Magyar 2014). To capture the ever-changing nature of life, he hopes the scanning process will help him to reach his goal. »I took the sensor out from a scanner. I put it behind a camera lens and made a software that allowed me to make a pretty good control for this project. Instead of moving a document in front of the sensor I let life moving in front of it and let life scanning itself on the images« (Magyar 2014).

Illustration 5: Adam Magyar. Stainless (video).

Source: http://www.magyaradam.com

Scanning becomes a way of measuring time. Everything is equal: the camera transforms reality; opposite movements let people walk backward in time. Magyar scans trains and people waiting for trains. He solves problems of shaking and light flickering through writing his own code. The software he designed removes nearly all distortions from his data, producing impressively clear imagery.

In Tokyo, New York, and Berlin train and subway stations, Magyar captures invisible moments and invisible things. High-speed photography allows him to catch instant something is not yet there, a movement that is a movement in its attempt, incredibly slow and beautiful (Magyar 2011, Cade 2014, Hammer 2014).

THINGS LOOKING BACK—DRONES / REMOTES / MACHINES

»The DIY Drone Brigade puts the ominous tools of state power into the hands of the people. We are the operators. We are the eyes in the skies. Join us to explore ubiquitous surveillance culture in our global back yard!« (DIY Drone Brigade n.d.)

Originally a drone was a male honeybee, but after 2010 the word became better known as the name for an unmanned mobile device. Drones were originally military tools, unmanned small remote-controlled planes used for surveillance or pinpoint attacks. They were primarily used in situations where normal military gear and personnel would be unable to go. It is an ideal tool for surveillance of the city jungle as well.

Chungking Express as a cinema drama was constructed on the jungle of the city. With the movie we discover the truth of love in that jungle, the thousands of corners, millions of people, cars and objects. The drones are tools developed for areas that have no fixed surveillance points. The jungle of the city seems to be surveilled 24/7 but still has hidden areas, holes unreachable by the surveilling machinery.

If we can look at anything surrounding us with and through our tools, then drones are a new category of things that look back at us. In the Internet of things, any kind of device or thing can surveil its environment. A fridge can surveil its contents; a car can surveil the road, the direction it's going, surrounding traffic, its speed. The car can also learn from its user: the habitual way she moves and operates the vehicle. Anything in any way can look back at us. Unlike the military drone, there doesn't need to be a human operator. It could be a software routine or loop, registering and performing.

Drones are an obvious remote gaze. In 2013, the Occupy movement met the maker movement—DIY met the military. More and more do-it-yourself drone sites gave instructions on how to build and operate quadcopters and other flying objects. A driving force was of course the thrill of being able to create aerial photographs and aerial videos, to fly over one's living places and watch oneself from above. The GoPro camera and the video abilities of smartphones make it simple to construct lightweight carriers and flying vehicles. What had been a domain of the military and professional photographers has now become accessible to the general public, geeks and amateurs, who can now create astonishing imagery.

»Slowly, but increasingly definitively, our technologies and our devices are learning to see, to hear, to place themselves in the world. Phones know their location by GPS. Financial algorithms read the news and feed that knowledge back into the market. Everything has a camera in it. We are becoming acquainted with new ways of seeing: the Gods-eye view of satellites, the Kinect's inside-out sense of the living room, the elevated car-sight of Google Street View, the facial obsessions of CCTV.« (SxSW 2012).

While small, lightweight cameras and drones are clearly visible (at least so far) technological objects, other tools are appearing that actually make things see. The Microsoft Kinect is another kind of a technological transfer from the military and intelligence fields to the public. »WW2 and ballistics gave us digital computers. Cold War decentralization gave us the Internet. Terrorism and mass surveillance: Kinect« (Borenstein 2012).

The Kinect sensor resembles a technology that was developed to detect terrorists in public spaces through facial recognition, gait analysis, skeletonization, and most of all depth imaging. With the Kinect, gestural interfaces can be developed to control objects on screens simply through gestures or body movements. With its built-in camera and infrared sensors, the Kinect can scan 3D objects for cheap reproduction, and it supports motion capture for 3D character animation. The Kinect is a tool that for the first time makes a consumer computer really see what is around it.

»While we've been able to use computers to process still images and video for decades, simply iterating over red, green, and blue pixels misses most of the amazing capabilities that we take for granted in the human vision system: seeing in stereo, differentiat- ing objects in space, tracking people over time and space, recognizing body language, etc. For the first time, with this revolution in camera and image- processing technology, we're starting to build computing applications that take these same capabilities as a starting point. And, with the arrival of the Kinect, the ability to create these applications is now within the reach of even weekend tinkerers and casual hackers.« (Borenstein 2012)

MACHINE VISION

»It's 2011 and I Have No Idea What Anything Is or What It Does Anymore« (Bridle 2011). This was the subtitle for James Bridle's keynote address to Web Directions South 2011, *Waving at the Machines*. Bridle describes what he calls »New Aesthetics,« a project about new ways of seeing and the aesthetics resulting from them, »new styles and senses«, which »recur in our art, our designs, and our products« as a result of devices and technology that can see, hear, and place themselves in our world.

With a wide range of examples, observations, and phenomena Bridle describes how we have entered into a dialogue with technology and the machinery we created. The world we are living in and that we are seeing, we are seeing through satellites, digitally through cameras, mediated through technology. Our memories are based on the technology they are connected and related with. We can foresee a future where we enter a room and say hello, waving to identify ourselves because the room, the computers and the machines are watching us. Bridle's talk sounds like a Ray Bradbury story, but it's here. We already share our world with things that are watching us, and we are in dialogue with these things. As Bridle says, »it can be creepy and it can be surveillance, or it can be shared vision« (Bridle 2011).

Bridle closed with a series of finger paintings by Evan Roth.[2] These paintings are based on gestures we make on touchscreens when we type in our user name and password or slide to unlock a screen. The paintings document gestures no human being has made before. These gestures are mediated through the technology we are using in our lives and in the world we inhabit.

Technology shapes our behavior and our vision. The clips we create are negotiations of how the world relates to things and us. The video-enabled devices we use are part of what we want to be and part of what technology wants to be as well.

Booka Shade, an electronic music act from Germany, released a video to their 2014 single *Crossing Borders* shot by a drone with seven GoPro Hero cameras attached. The video, which is polished and glossy like house music, was directed by Ryan Stake, and the drone cinematography was by Octofilms (Aguilar 2014). The seven GoPros create an amazing landscape effect of unique locations mapped on a globe with beautiful distortions, stretching and squeezing something like a multiple-viewpoint or panoramic perspective of objects, architecture, and nature. Vertical shapes, textures, and patterns, both built and natural, are taken from flight with a full pano-

---

2   See http://www.evan-roth.com/work/multi-touch-finger-paintings/

ramic 360-degree angle and rendered in the single rhythmical image flow of the music video.

»Remember: Drones might be up in the sky all by themselves, but in a lot of cases there's a totally freaked out human being operating the machines from earth« (Aguilar 2014).

*

Czech-born philosopher Villem Flusser, who wrote extensively about photography, addressed the relationship between camera and operator:

»The camera is an apparatus which was programmed to make pictures. The photographer is expected to act within that program. If he does so, he will be making pictures of the outside world. That world reflects rays, which the camera captures on sensitive surfaces, and the photographer who acts within the camera program will 'document' the outside world as captured by the camera. But the photographer may refuse to act within the camera program. He may transfer his interest from the outside world toward the camera interior. He may concentrate upon what happens to the rays, which come into the camera from the outside world. The pictures, which such a photographer will produce will no longer 'document' the outside world, but rather the camera program. They will thus whiten the black box. Such pictures are important, because the camera program, which they show, is one among the many apparatus programs, which are about to structure our perceptions, desires, feelings, our knowledges and our actions. In fact: such a photographer who refuses to go by the camera program is committed to showing the hidden programs of the emerging society of automatic apparatus.« (Flusser 1995)

BEYONCE VERTICAL

> It has been demonstrated that all species of life on earth that have become extinct were doomed through overspecialization, whether anatomical, biological, or geological. Therefore conventional narrative cinema, in which the filmmaker plays policeman guiding our eyes here and there in the picture plane, might be described as „specialized vision," which tends to decay our ability to comprehend the more complex and diffuse visual field of living reality.
>
> GENE YOUNGBLOOD/EXPANDED CINEMA

AUTHENTICITY

Authenticity is the truthfulness of origins, attributions, commitments, sincerity, devotion, and intentions.

The year 2012, when the world should have ended, passed. The usual entertainment programs are running on television. The big event before the unavoidable Victoria's Secret fashion show on New Year's Eve is a concert by the American singer Beyoncé. The Turkish TV channel CNBCe screens it at 3 in the morning. We might already have learned of Beyoncé's private concert in Las Vegas that same night for only 700 selected guests. Nevertheless, there is Beyoncé for everyone. Now, globally, we are invited to share the event with her through the TV broadcast. We are part of the story. We are not waiting outside. Like sold-out national soccer games projected in public spaces European cities for a cheering crowd, we are sharing a public screening and being together.

At one moment of the broadcast, the program cuts from the stage, with its a normal formatted television image, to a vertical slot-like image in the horizontal center of the television. Grayish black fills the sides of the image on widescreen TVs. The image doesn't just *seem* like a video from a mobile phone, it *is* one. The phone is recording while its owner holds it vertically. The vertical image, shaky and walking toward Beyoncé, allows us to participate in a much more intimate environment. We are backstage and we are experiencing a spontaneous self-performance of Beyoncé.

The flow of the concert has slowed down to an intimate and private moment, a moment of chill out, meditation, and relaxing, listening to a single voice and watching a single person's privacy in her rehearsal and self-reflexiveness.

But this mobile phone-like footage that we are seeing on CNBCe on New Year's Eve 2012 is not from the Las Vegas concert—this is a video from May 2011 recorded during the television show *American Idol*. Jay-Z, Beyoncé's husband, recorded the video backstage.

In the video, she's accompanied by her family, her closest friends and colleagues, band members, and background singers. She is obviously working on her new song *1+1*, which she will perform live on stage a short time later. Her voice seems to be authentic. The situation seems to be authentic. The vertical video and its grayish-black stripes at the sides document and help to increase the authenticity of the intimate situation.

This is the situation, the story Jay-Z refers to in a May 2011 comment under the video: »Sometimes you need perspective. You've been right in front of greatness so often that you need to step back and see it again for the first time. This is the dressing room rehearsal for American Idol. NO MICROPHONE. No effects. – Andy WarHOV« (Life+Times 2011).

But why does Beyoncé need authenticity? Why is there a need for such a video? And why could it be important that this video is vertical?

Beyoncé is haunted. She is haunted by her own image, the image she would like to create and to be in public, the image of a perfectionist, the singer, the artist. In January 2013 the inauguration of Barack Obama once again threw a shadow on her successful career progression from the girl group Destiny's Child to the Beyoncé of today: She was singing along with a prerecorded track.

Her show at halftime of American football's Super Bowl in 2012, with the reappearance of the other members of Destiny's Child at her side, had pushed her into the stratosphere of pop music, but the inauguration playback again prompted questions of whether she could really sing.

In the rehearsal video, being shot with a mobile phone and being vertical constructs the authenticity of the intimate event and her ability to sing, underlining and responding to the belief in popular culture that a singer no longer needs to be able to sing to be a successful pop star. The video's verticality refers to the amateurish act and response to the moment of experience, something that is not controlled and presumes to be witnessed.

This kind of construction of authenticity is similar to a common approach to documentary filmmaking, as Florian Schneider wrote in 2013:

»A conventional notion of the documentary is based on the idea to keep reality firmly and fix in order to play them back in the future. A special moment or specific point can be identified, isolated, transferred to a neutral storage medium and as an event reconstructed in such a way that ideological forms of truth are generated, which with their respective conditionality's should have some, though not necessarily predictable, inventory in time and space.« (Schneider 2013)[1]

Schneider suggests further that documentary image creation is part of a postindustrial creation of fiction. In this case, the vertical video of Beyoncé's rehearsal is part of an already existing fiction and further fictionalization of the pop star. The form of the video and its image aspect ratio become part of the process—its verticalness restricts the view, takes attention to its content, the movement of the recording person and the view through a slot. The video never shows us the entire backstage area. It goes from person to person and ends with Beyoncé in a corner alone. It could be anywhere and anytime.

Conventionally, a filmmaker would frame the outside within the inside of the frame; conversely, the audience would automatically expand the room as it's framed and complete its fragmented view. The vertical shot does not allow this completeness, restricting viewers to the internal fiction. Therefore, it is completed in itself and includes a reality that is just the real-

---

1 Translation from German is mine.

ity inside of the frame and not any other expanding and surrounding. We know who is around and with Beyoncé as the video guides us, but the video does not show us anything else, and therefor there is no idea of proof included in the video.

While the camera moves with its owner through the space, the space unfolds for the viewer as a poor narrative space. The narrative is the narrative of witnessing privacy, peeping through a hole, but permitted and guided. It's a carnivalesque operation. The vertical video image masks another possible video image, another possible frame, but that frame would have been less narrative—it would have been just and only real. The vertical video covers what would be otherwise visible, but it does this to construct a narrative out of the limit of the vertical image. The normal video or the widescreen video would have continued the known narrative of disbelief, but the vertical video shifts the narrative, magnifying an emotional reaction of the fans.

VERTICAL VIDEO SYNDROME—SHAPE SHIFTING

The Beyoncé video is part of an Internet phenomenon that was developing in 2011 and came to be called the Vertical Video Syndrome in 2012. Videos shot with video-enabled mobile phones are usually shot vertical. In June 2012, the Glove and Boots YouTube channel uploaded a video titled *Vertical Video Syndrome – A PSA* (Glove and Boots 2012). The public service announcement by *Glove and Boots* features the puppets Maria and Fafa talking about a serious problem. They and other puppets are complaining about videos shot in portrait orientation.

In the opening of the video we see an unhappy gorilla puppet in front of a wall with a portrait of the smiling Hollywood actor John Goodman framed between two big black areas in the YouTube viewer. The gorilla turns to the audience and makes a grumpy sound. A sentimental piano melody starts playing. Another puppet, Fafa the groundhog, enters the black area to the right of the gorilla and begins talking:

»This video didn't have to look this way. It could have been prevented.«

The gorilla looks to the right to the groundhog puppet.

»Say no to vertical videos!« Fafa continues. The gorilla turns to the audience. The puppet Mario enters from the left, and the gorilla turns to him. Mario: »Vertical videos happen when you hold your camera the wrong way. Your video will end up looking like grab.«

Fafa describes the phenomenon known as Vertical Video Syndrome in detail; categorizing people treating videos like pictures or don't even care. The puppet refers to cinema and television, which have always been horizontal. Computer screens and our eyes are horizontal arranged.

Fafa says, »We aren't built to watch vertical videos.«
If people continue to produce vertical videos, the dramatic side effects would be that YouTube would play four videos next to each other to save bandwidth. And if the »disease« spreads further, cinemas will become "»tall and skinny.« The theaters will need to be rebuilt.

Mario says, »and George Lucas will rerelease Star Wars again. The skinny addition.«

The video cuts with a comic whoop sound effect from the puppets to a masked video with a center vertical rectangle of George Lucas, where you see only one half of his face and a hand.

Lucas says, »I was never really able to tell the story that I wanted to tell. This is a great chance for me to experiment with a new technology.«

The video of the puppets has several million views and more than 8000 comments as of early 2014. In spring 2014, Google released an application on its new phone that seems like an extended reaction to the puppets video. The new app, which has impressive features like fake-bokeh lens blur and a 50MP high-resolution photo sphere, also automatically detects if a user is holding the phone vertically (that is, in the »wrong« orientation), and an icon pops up to remind the user to turn it horizontal (Cade 2014). The icon recalls the puppets Mario and Fafa's »you're not shooting that right dummy!« and as noted by Cade, Google's camera app takes on the war against vertical video.

Of course, a simple explanation of why people shoot vertical videos is the ease and quickness of a one-hand use of mobile phones and especially smartphones to take a single photo. It is actually a consequence of product and interface design. The home buttons on the phone and in applications fit the thumb perfectly. The same movements—moving the thumb over the screen to select the app, pressing the home or release button—are required to snap a photo or record a video.

Video on the iPhone is only one slide away from the photographic mode. A quick video can therefore be shot very fast with no setup: just one hand and very little movement. To take a horizontal video with the iPhone, the user needs to orient the phone horizontally with one hand. The handheld operation is difficult, and it's even more difficult to tap the screen or release the recording button. The phone and application appear out of balance. Intuitive use will result in touching record while the phone is lying comfortable in one's hand.

The operation of shooting a movie with the same device, of course, would consequently relate to an organized and controlled event in which the content, the shooting distance, and the aspect ratio of the video are already decided. The spontaneity of vertical videos might just be their charming point, and their legitimation as being closer to real life comes through their intuitiveness.

Shooting video with one hand and one button, paired with the ability to share the recordings easily, is nothing new. In April 2011, Cisco Systems officially announced the end of the Flip video camera business and the end of its life support. The Flip camera was a small one-button video camera that was easy to operate with one hand because of its vertical construction and its one-button operation, but it shot a horizontal aspect ratio. The Flip Video Ultra camera in 2008 was the highlight of affordable, one-button pocket-size video camcorders. It could record YouTube-ready video, meaning that they were shot according to YouTube's technical standards. With its USB connection, the Flip camera was easy to connect to a computer to upload, share, or store the videos. Compared with the abilities of smartphones, which have multiple functions and tasks embedded and are immediately connected to a network for upload or streaming, the Flip camera was a kind of intermediary product in the transfer of technology to the consumer market. Cisco might have simply discontinued the product for various reasons: because of competition from other companies and the growth of video-enabled smartphones, but also just for operational business reasons as the company's main business is not the consumer market (Warren 2011, Flip Video 2014).

In a February 2013 blog post, James Watt asks why people are so upset about vertical videos.

»There seems to be a consensus among the "Internet Elite" that all vertical videos are rubbish and should be stricken from the Earth. It has become Internet culture groupthink to vehemently disapprove of these videos. Does the average member of the herd even understand why they are to disapprove of vertical videos? Or, do they just repeat and reinforce the same culture conformity banter they've seen elsewhere?« (Watt 2013)

According to Google statistics of search interests, the fictitious disease of Vertical Video Syndrome did not appear on the web before June 2012, when the puppet video was released (Google Search Trends 2012). By the time Watt wrote his defense of the practice, vertical video had become a known Internet meme. For Watt, the main reason for the unrest and the satirical suppression of vertical video was simply that YouTube was unable to embed them proper and display them correctly without black sides in a horizontal field.

»A large portion of crazy videos that go viral are recorded vertically. When you're standing in public, recording something vertically helps conceal your actions. Plus, a landscape shot of the scene doesn't add any additional information. "Here's a video of some guy going nuts. I know how important viral video quality is to the Internet, so I recorded it horizontally. Yeah, that means I cut off half his body, but look at that pavement and grass I got in the background!"
Besides being inconspicuous and providing a better aspect ratio in certain situations, vertical videos will continue to remain popular simply because more people own phones than ever before. People who are "unplugged" from Internet culture will continue to record however they want.
As I said before, the original reason for disliking vertical videos was problems with playback. Let's also keep in mind that most people are not watching phone-recorded, widescreen YouTube videos in full screen. It should become immediately clear who is to blame for vertical videos: YouTube! Not the person who created the vertical video!« (Watt 2013)

Vimeo, seen as a more professional and ambitious video-sharing site, allows users to upload their vertical videos and embed them without having black stripes. In its video school lectures, the site also engaged users to play with the aspect ratio and think about creative use of the portrait mode, transferring photographic practices into the realm of horizontal-dominated digital cinematography (Hooper 2012).

There is of course the classic argumentation that our visual field is horizontal and therefore cinematographic formats and screens are horizontal. Television transformed from a standard 4:3 aspect ratio to 16:9 widescreen with high definition digital video broadcast and the now developing 4k rounded screens. There might be 21:9 screens on the way, but other forms of screens are possible and are already deliverable in various device attachments. The widescreen format is still simply the demand of the movie production industry, which dominates the market of cinematic storytelling.

Framing Acts

In 2013, how someone holds a working smartphone can attest to her or his experience and cinematographic literacy, but it also establishes that the person grew up with pre-digital media forms, meaning analog cinema and television. Newer generations might not necessarily prefer a specific aspect ratio, as the aspect ratio of digital moving images might depend of the narrative universe and world they relate to.

People recording a video in a music concert might not care about the aspect ratio if they're shooting their video as a memory for their personal digital album or space on the phone or in a cloud, to be shared, tagged, and commented on. The moving image is a personal extraction out of the real experience. People don't think about framing. The extracted video defines a personalized center for the surrounding concert. The act of recording is accomplished with whatever tool is easy and available in that instant. The number of ways to post such videos has grown: YouTube videos, animated GIFs, Vines, Instagram, and on and on. The number of recording devices has grown as well: phones or Google Glass, but also tablet computers and other miniature personal computers (N. Jurgenson 2013a).

Vertical videos document situations of affect, and while doing so; they create a perceptive layer in hybrid events, arranging themselves near other type of videos. Multiple recordings with location information of concerts, gatherings, demonstrations, and protests like Gezi Park in 2013 in Istanbul build a virtual layer expanding the actual space of an event endlessly.

At the 2008 Video Vortex meeting, Sarah Kesenne, a Belgian researcher, emphasized the recording act of concert videos. She wrote about what she called *On Gig Flix* in the first Video Vortex Reader:

»What a thrill to see the videos Latin-American U2 fans uploaded on the web. They show the same Vertigo tour shows of the concert film 'U23D' I saw the evening before in Brussels' IMAX film venue. It is said to be the first 3-D multi-camera recording of a live event ever. All the muscles of this 85 minute immersive experience of tangible high definition, spectacular spidercam shots and graphic overlays contrast highly with the ephemeral qualities of these short, handheld 'cellflix' of Argentinian and Mexican teenagers. But they are both signs of our times. In one of these amateur videos we find our 15 years old cameraman laughing at the lens in extreme close-up, meanwhile joking to his friends. They're all waiting for the kick-off of the long expected U2 concert of the Vertigo tour. Night has fallen, and he sweeps his phone 360 grades around: a generic camera movement to express exposition. We get vaguely an idea of the enormous mass of people gathered in the football stadium, an average of 100 000 people according to the website of 'U23D'. We seem miles away from the stage. Now the blaring lights of this sports arena go out, and for a long time the quicktime player shows nothing but a black screen, if not for the glowing mobile screens, like dirty pixels. The start of the concert is pure ecstasy, and abstract: a distant light explosion and videowalls popping up in the dark. The phone returns to his pocket, while much closer to the action the 'U23D' crew gets its multi-camera set rolling. To achieve the 3-D stereoscopical effect, the concert is filmed simultaneously by a double camera apparatus: a grateful metaphor for the multiple video practices I want to discuss here.« (Kersenne 2011)

At the 9th Video Vortex conference in 2011, Italian researcher Vito Campanelli recalled the act of framing itself while asking how it changes in the transition to digital cameras, devices, and practices. Campanelli referred to Vilem Flusser's 1983 essay about photography and used it as his theoretical framework to isolate and analyze »two different attitudes, constitutive of the framing act«—posture and gesture.

»Both contribute to the characterization of the contemporary framing act, which, under the pressure of a variety of sociocultural and technological dynamics (which I have tried to enumerate), tends to become a game with the categories of video and photography, played out in a space already saturated with information.« (Campanelli 2013)

The automation of digital recording devices produces a sensation of domination toward the apparatus, a reduction in experimentation with time, and switches the emphasis toward a multitude of points of view. While temporal categories seem to disappear in this contemporary practice, spatial categories gain advantage. Digital editing possibilities and technologies make digital memories infinitely editable and produce a flow of variations. With higher resolution and complex image compressions, the framing act can even come later.

The former shooting and hunting metaphor of photography shifts toward posture and gesture. The usage of displays rather than viewfinder leads, according to Campanelli, to keeping a certain distance, and creates a new grammar of posture. The framing act becomes an elegant gesture through its aesthetization in the transition from viewfinder to display.

The contemporary framing act takes information to be real in itself, not just a container for meaning. It is an act of searching information around us, which makes it one of the numerous possibilities of interaction with the data overload that characterizes present time.

The framed video documents in any form or aspect ratio our inhabiting of social space and »reassembles« the space of information around us. The pleasure of framing documents the fight for space.

Depicting space is a gesture related to seeing what exists and therefore what is real around us. The multitude of frames and framing acts, combined with the overruling of defined aspect ratios, creates a completeness of view. In the simple photographic act, what was not framed did not exist, but in the multitude of gestures it is still possible to be. Therefore, as Campanelli says, posture and gesture document a continuously growing world existence for us. Since our physical world cannot grow anymore, our video world can.

Vertical Cinema

We are tempted to compare our vision with cinematic reality and cinematic experience with our vision. It is a measurable fact that our horizontal field of vision is expanded and our vertical field limited. Cinema moved toward a more horizontal screen in the fight against television, leaving its standard and nearly square format of the 1.33:1 or 4:3 aspect ratio. The history of the moving image is defined through standards set based on the mechanical abilities of reproduction. With digital devices and screens, aspect ratio becomes a matter of design decisions, user functions, and user abilities as well as technical conditions. The moving image is adaptable to various forms. Vertical video appears with and through the recording device. The device image resists the forces of compositional standards and traditions, following aesthetics of interface dominated by marketing interests and needs. The Hollywood frame is totally managed and calculated, in opposition to the spontaneous posture and gesture of hand, device, and eyes in distance. The Hollywood frame produces an inside and outside world through its strict aesthetic conditions, immersing the audience in a dominant narrative, whereas the device image emerges out of a perceived reality, constructed through the device, but project in a space beyond.

»Arnheim argues that the frame of a shot imposes a limitation on what can be seen by the film viewer that 'in the actual range of human vision … simply does not exist.' This is because our eyes, heads, and bodies are 'mobile.' Hence, 'the field of vision is in practice unlimited and infinite.' We can move our eyes, heads, and bodies to see what is at any one moment out of sight, beyond the periphery of our vision. But 'it is otherwise with the film or photograph,' for the frame of a still shot prevents us from seeing what lies beyond the edge of the frame…. Hence, film diverges from mechanical reproduction because the frame of a shot restricts what we can see, and no such restriction obtains in normal perceptual experience.« (Turvey 2010)

Aspect ratio and the frame itself are already part of the history of material experimentation in experimental film. Setting themselves in a history of experimental film, in 2013 a group of 10 filmmakers created a film festival event based on the idea of a vertical screen and a vertical 35mm film projection. In February 2014, the program was presented at the Stedelijk museum in Amsterdam and accompanied by lectures setting the framework of the artistic endeavor after sold-out screenings at the 2014 International Film Festival in Rotterdam. What started in Austria in 2013 has become a European move toward a vertical extended screen as a form of art.²

The vertical cinema screen demands a vertical architecture that allows narrow and high projection. It is obvious that historically churches in Europe were built accordingly with their sacral areas. Vertical cinema sets itself in a parallel condition, a religious act of cinema and moving image culture. The audience close to the screen needs to lie down to enjoy the vertically extending moving image. The screening itself consists of abstract imagery, formal experiments, found footage, live laser action captured on film, and immersive soundscapes.

»What we usually identify as the indisputable 'temple of film', the Cinema, is not really a given, especially not in the realm of experimental cinematic arts. Yet this is somehow sidelined in the process of re-thinking the possibilities of cinematic experience, mostly because the architectural frame is already there, if only as a convention established a long time ago within the theatrical arts. Actually, the history of experimental cinema and the art of the moving image suggests that the space might very well be the crucial aspect of the total audiovisual experience—something one should always question and take into consideration when producing a work for audiovisual, sensory cinema.
For the Vertical Cinema project we 'abandoned' traditional cinema formats, opting instead for cinematic experiments that are designed for projection in a tall, narrow space. It is not an invitation to leave cinemas—which have been radically transformed over the past decade according to the diktat of the commercial film market—but a provocation to expand the image onto a new axis. This project re-thinks the actual projection space and returns it to the filmmakers. It proposes a future for filmmaking rather than a pessimistic debate over the alleged death of film.« (Vertical Cinema n.d.)

---

2 The first showing of Vertical Cinema at the Kontraste Festival Krems in Austria in October 2013. The event was held at the church of Grey Friars, a venue typically used for music performances. (Markus Gradwohl)

Even the creators of the program extensively refer to cinema and the history of experimental film; the form of their presentations, combined with loud, often rhythmic static and bright light patterns, recalls VJ shows in clubs and installations of visual music works, separating itself from video mapping activities and works or world exhibition pavilions with multiple screens and projections. The 90 degree turned cinemascope moving image combined with architecture and soundscape creates a Wagnerian sensory overload, a total work of art in the combination of image, audio, and architecture.

TYRANNY OF THE FRAME

»We view all the plastic arts through a rigid frame. Since painting separated itself from architecture at the end of the Medieval period, it regulated its parameters, with very little exception, to fit four right-angles. And theater, with a proscenium arch, copied painting; opera and ballet arranged its scenarios and choreography to be seen in association with theatre's proscenium arch stage-space, and cinema copied the theatre, and television copied the cinema, and then there are photographs squared up for painting-picture-frames and to fit the right angles of a book. This wholesale practice has become so traditional and orthodox, it is not questioned.« (Greenaway 2003)

In his militant 1983 lecture, Peter Greenaway more or less declares that we are conditioned by the view through a window. Traditional cinema and traditional film theory started thinking of the cinema screen as a window to a parallel universe to be experienced by the audience in the cinema salon. Till the 19th century and the invention of cinema, the major aspect ratio of windows could not match the modern screen.

Greenaway emphasizes that no frame exists in nature. The frame is a man-made device. It is a regulation of our own irregular experience of our view on the world around us. The only borders we feel are our cheekbones when we keep our head and eyes steady.

»It is an ironic curiosity that the Japanese have tried to reverse the game by forcing man-devised frames into landscape design using the sea horizon as the absolute horizontal, and planting tall straight-trunked trees to make the vertical frame-lines— ironic and curious, since Oriental picture-making has steadfastly, until it came in contact with Western practices of seeing, eschewed the frame, not finding it at all necessary to use a frame to contain and shape the world.« (Greenaway 2003)

In 1983, of course, Greenaway was unaware of practices that would follow 30 years later, but in his argumentation against the frame and against the 4:3 television image restriction, he makes the point that cinema even in its experimental forms always had been tightened. Instead of adapting the moving image toward televised frames, he suggests that we un-create the frame—that we simply get rid of it.

TIME FRAMES

With vertical videos embedded in websites, other graphical forms are gaining narrative and time-shaping emphasis, as they appear on a screen simultaneously. The overall view of graphical framed objects builds relations that suggest other structural conditions than just sequential ones. They suggest simultaneity and a time relation inside the multiple frames or between them in the *gutter*, as the space is called in comics. As the single video is represented through a *keyframe* or running in a viewer representing a rectangular graphic shape, we transfer our attention to other elements of the same view, thus spending time.

Ignoring the constant update of spatial relationship with the moving image and taking it as a static element that is part of a kind of page view of a screen in totality at one moment in time, it seems to be helpful to compare the appearance and the perception of such a screen with the practice of reading and experiencing a graphic novel or comic.

Will Eisner, in *Comics and Sequential Art*, describes the experience of duration as an integral dimension to sequential art (Eisner 1985). Eisner links to the idea that time is combined with space and sound. They are interdependent. Movements and actions are meaningful and perceived in their relationship to each other. Time is an illusory factor measured through our experience. In comics it is a structural element. Timing for Eisner is the arrangement of graphical elements.

»In the modern comic strip or comic book, the device most fundamental to the transmission of timing is the panel or frame or box. These lines drawn around the depiction of a scene, which act as a containment of the action, have as one of their functions the task of separating or parsing the total statement.« (Eisner 1985, 28)

In comics, panels are specifically used for timing and therefore storytelling. Small or short panels create speed and hasten reading, »whereas medium panels evoke a sense of pacing. They let the story flow and characters develop. Large, full-page panels are for an effect. Usually one of shock« (Deering 2000).

Scott McCloud, certainly influenced by Will Eisner, explains in *Understanding Comics* the relation of time and frame as each panel shows a single moment of time. When we read, we fill in the time and movement between the single moments or single panels, creating the illusion of passing time. Paradoxically, panels are graphical objects that are placed side by side in a spatial domain, but as they follow each other or are read one after another, their domain is also time. In the succession of images or panels, comics are able to include past, present, and future in one compositional unit, unifying time in one space. A single panel can in combination with words or text also have several layers of time following a string of reading convention.

»The panels are moments and they contain time that is distributed on the page with the white gaps as dividers that keep the time and designates when one moment ends and the next begins—neat little squares of time laid out like pearls on a string. Though often times in comics, images provide some sort of spatial anchorage for the narrative, they often also contribute to the temporality. And vice versa. Text in comics can help temporalize an image, as Scott McCloud illustrates … but text often also provides clues and information about the spatial properties of the action or lack thereof. Movements progress in time, and for this reason the indication of movement made by speed lines in a panel can suggest temporality through the use of this comics-specific convention…. In much the same way that speed lines suggest time but are not actually time, the images of comics also suggest a three-dimensional space through their two-dimensional representations.« (Corsten 2012)

McCloud's central statement on time and space in comics is that we all have learned to perceive time spatially. In the world of comics, according to McCloud, time and space are one and the same (Corsten 2012).

»As with many of Scott McCloud's propositions from his much discussed work Understanding Comics—which is a theory of comics in the form of comics—this assertion about the nature of time and space in comics appears intuitively to be correct, especially because of the elegant way he visually illustrates this quote, with his comics alter ego walking along a ruler which is then smoothly converted into a clock. A measurement for spatial units is simultaneously a measuring instrument for temporal units and, accordingly, space and time are the same. The experience of reading comics involves time and space, and their relation, in very complicated ways, and there is to a certain extent an experience of perceiving time spatially.« (Corsten 2012, 40)

In her reflection of time and space in comics, Rikke Platz Cortsen questions McCloud's argument that time and space are divers concepts and asks for a deeper reflection. Because panels are laid out spatially on a page and show only a moment in a story, McCloud argues that time is presented spatially and becomes space. Will Eisner described the arrangement of panels as a way of conveying a sense of time. As Cortsen points out, Eisner refers to an illusion of time rather than the concept of time.

Thierry Groensteen introduces the concept of multiframe to be able to divide the various kinds of spaces involved in a comic. The multiframe »allows us to imagine a contentless comic, 'cleansed' of its iconic and verbal contents, and constructed as a finished series of supporting frames—in short, a comic provisionally reduced to its spatio-topical parameters« (Corsten 2012).

Groensteen distinguishes further between hyperframes and multiframes:

»The notions of the hyperframe and the multiframe must not be confused. The notion of the hyperframe applies itself to a single unit, which is that of the page. The forms of the multiframe on the other hand, are multiple. (...) If one wishes, it is possible to speak of the simple multiframe that is the page, or of every unit of lesser rank that joins several panels (the half page or the strip). Piling up the printed pages on the recto and the verso, the book itself constitutes a paged multiframe.« (Corsten 2012)

The hyperframe determines how the panels are placed or structured on a page. The panels have characteristics like form, shape, area, size, and site or location on the page. These are spatial distinction independent of the content. By emphasizing these parameters of the panels, disruption or various kinds of relations can be constructed. The constructed space might then differ from the narrated space. In other words, the represented space differs from the space of representation. The space is no longer just simply one space, as Cortsen points out.

»Comics panels fracture both time and space, offering a jagged, staccato rhythm of unconnected moments. But closure allows us to connect these moments and mentally construct a continuous, unified reality« (Corsten 2012).

LET'S GET VERTICAL

»My brother Joe and a painting he is working on.« is the content description of a video shared around 2012 on Vimeo under the title *Let's get vertical* (Zappile 2012). The video appeared in a Google search for a video with the same title by Vimeo's own video school. This video has very few views and seems to have been intended as private. What is interesting is that the vertical video is split into three panels like a comic. The vertical video itself becomes a hyperframe with first two and then three frames within the frame becoming parallel moments of time of a past and present where Joe is painting, ending with a single panel of the painting.

The video underlines the continuity of painting in Joe's life. It also emphasizes and strengthens the process. The resulting painting is illustrated by the foregoing multitude of painting. The process is aestheticized.

A similar image process aesthetic that especially underlines the character of *process* can be found in the television series *CSI* (*Crime Scene Investigation*) and its various offshoots set in New York, Las Vegas, or Miami. Whenever the lab is shown at work or one of the members of the lab is following an investigative laboratory procedure, the screen is split. Multiframes show multiple states of the same process at the same time. This not only shortens the time of the process, but also functions as intensive documentation and beautification of effort and technology.

The parallel panels with multiple times in one hyperframe create an intensification of the actual moment of perception and presentation for the viewer in the context of the viewed, recalling David Bordwell's observation of intensified continuity in cinema.

INTERIORS & EXTERIORS

> I often think of video as a dense three-dimensional matrix, as is customary in the computer vision community. Width and height contain the image, and a moving image has a temporal element, giving the form depth. The video can be frozen into a cubic block, and subject to what stretching, cutting, carving, and patching would seem fit for a cube.
> ROBERT OCHSHORN

CINEMA REDUX

Thumber is a little not-so-fresh Mac software application that was last released in 2008, which allows watching a full movie at once. In one-second intervals, the application takes snapshots from a Quicktime video and stitches them together into one image from left to right and top to bottom (Thumber n.d.). The *Thumber* image can then be printed as a huge movie poster, allowing us to look at once inside a movie. Based on Brandon Dawes' concept work *Cinema Redux*, *Thumber* creates a visual fingerprint of each movie. Brandon Dawes created *Cinema Redux* in 2004, and Museum of Modern Art (MoMA) in New York acquired it in 2008 (Dawes 2008). In his original artwork, the resulting image consists of 60 frames in each row of one-minute film time taken in one-second intervals. As a »visual distillation« of an entire movie, the resulting image is unique for every film. Every single moment is brought together in one single entity or new object. We can see the movie at once, see its flow or past, get an idea about its story development. Fast cuts appear with fast changes in color and brightness when viewed from a distance, and when much closer we can see the change of single frames or panel content.

What Brandon Dawes does is simply to compress a film to a single image while keeping the essential inner visual information of time and flow, of change. It is possible to reconstruct the movie because of the images embedded and retained. This is a methodology that transfers data compression from one medium into another, here from a time-based medium to a two-dimensional print medium, paper, while keeping its temporal relation in a transformation of spatio-temporal relation. The space of the images is renewed and set into a relation with a hyper panel or frame and multi panels or frames embedded.

Because each *Thumber* image or *Cinema Redux* image is unique, it creates a visual identity for every film. Difference of images in time becomes a unique stamp and allows new forms of viewing at once and in detail as well as comparison and creates new sets of visual data. Of course, the form of data compression applied is lossy. Some data of the films has been lost. The resulting data is itself a unique set. The lossy compressed data is distilled or extracted from the original data to create a new form. In its material substance it is still related and able to assist in a reconstruction of the source film, but it cannot fill the gaps.

Compression as a form of distillation separates components. It is a material operation of data separation. With the separated data, other objects can be created. Even the process of data compression lets sets of data disappear forever, but the distilled data can become a new source set or code for new objects, even movies.

In this case of *Thumber*, our understanding of a movie as a whole is challenged and collapsed in several time levels at once. We are reconstructing a film out of the substance of the film. The film reconstructed cannot be the source—it is an object with spatio-temporal similarities. For every viewer, the compressed image is also a unique experience of flow, space, and time. The compressed, extracted data set creates on a graphical level a new film. For some viewers, this film might be more meaningful than the original movie it was extracted from.

In our nature distillation or extraction of materials is common. Oils are extracted from olives. The olives are squeezed, and a liquid mixture is separated. Alcohol has been distilled for thousands of years. We use physical processes of separation to gain substances and materials that are useful to us. In the past, a digital compressed video image was something that looked jacky, edgy, with huge squared pixels visible as artifacts. It is generally considered that compression should be invisible, and the less a compression is visible the more it is successful.

As resolutions and video data sets are growing in detail, information and video compression technology advances constantly, keeping the appearance of the video image smooth and free of visual artifacts. These technologies might also be used to apply traditional analog methodologies or to transfer these into the digital. In that sense, one could use compression not just to make a set of data smaller and adjustable, and to use resources and storages more effective or enjoy transfer capacities, but to recreate new related sets of the extracted, resolving data.

In the analog world, video as a technological relative of television is or was simply a signal consisting of a single dot moving in a line from the left to the right of an invisible grid and from top to bottom and then starting again from the top left corner, creating the image through the speed of movement. In the digital world, the image is again a set of data of pixels as defined locations in a grid and the reading of it as a coded movement and time component. Video is defined in such a structure or corset. Compression of video could be seen as a way to filter mathematically the set of data and to break up the restrictions of the set video to construct a way of seeing from the inside through its digital materiality. A single clip of video could embed a complete world. Construction of meaning in cinema was created through the assemblage of shots, so editing could be defined as the lining up of clips in meaningful context. Compression, as the extraction of essence or substance of video data, could be another form of interior meaning creation.

COMPRESSIONS

The clips we watch on the Internet are squeezed, compressed into smaller file sizes for faster distribution. The speed of digital communication depends on compression. The quality and method of compression are a filtering force. Any information is selected and analyzed to discover what information can be eliminated to reduce file size. Compression of images, photographs, and movie files relates to the sensitivity of the human eye. Color information and dark areas are strongly reduced in details, as we are less sensitive to the amount of information.

Compression is an essential theme in the coding practice and works of Robert M. Ochshorn. Ochshorn offers a possibility to look inside a video clip by problematizing compression. In 2012, he demonstrated in a work for a documentary filmmaker a presentation of fifteen Godard films in one screen in a webpage. Each of the films is compressed to one horizontal line. An algorithm analyzing discontinuities segmented the films automatically into cuts. When the user moves the mouse over a cut, a playable image preview is launched. The selected film plays through its preview presentation image. The interface allows random play of the films. Clips can also be scattered across the screen on the basis of their colors. The prototype interface was written in HTML5 and Javascript for the web (Ochshorn 2012).

»Considered as a filtering protocol, the idea of compression can be applied more broadly to the production of moving images: editing a film entails a "compression" of many hours of footage into a comparatively short piece. In many cases, this compression too is deemed successful when it is imperceptible. The final result of editing should appear "complete" even though it is obviously missing most of what was filmed (not to mention what was never even recorded in the first place). And how few people there are who determine the parameters of compression—the relative importance of information—for so many! Compression of information into video is highly centralized. Directly between the social and technical compression of the moving picture is the editing interface: it is designed to facilitate the social process of compression and then perform an additional level of algorithmic compression to finally yield a form suitable for dissemination. And unsurprisingly its structure mirrors and re-enforces the social structure in which it operates: it is designed for use by a single operator to determine a canonical subset of closely-guarded, privately-held, source video for 'read-only' distribution to a passive audience.
It is at this site of production, the video editing interface, where I have started a multifaceted investigation into *compression*, in particular as concerns the organization and distribution of media.« (Ochshorn 2012)

For compression of video clips we need the data from every pixel in time, so while stretching the video in itself, the video offers a more random and user-related relation to a single moment in an archived event, which is actually a video in the form of a download.

»I often think of video as a dense three-dimensional matrix, as is customary in the computer vision community. Width and height contain the image, and a moving image has a temporal element, giving the form depth. The video can be frozen into a cubic block, and subject to what stretching, cutting, carving, and patching would seem fit for a cube. Of course as with all things digital, representation is ever-negotiable. From the perspective of an image sensor on a camcorder, each individual pixel over time could reasonably be seen as a one-dimensional stream, like an audio wave, and so you could imagine breaking apart the cube into millions of single-pixel streams. And it works in that you can reconstruct the cube from these streams, you can recreate the illusion of a moving picture. But viability of reconstruction is hardly a stringent criteria for representation.

I have been studying *compression* as a framework for thinking about meaning in a representation. There are two fundamental types of compressions: lossless, and lossy, meaning that the reconstruction of a compressed signal is either exactly as before the compression, in the former case, or close to the original in the latter. Lossless compression tends to operate on a byte stream of raw, digital data, and is effectively numerology—assorted number games to weed out redundancy—while lossy compression asserts a model of importance so that less important information can be discarded. For video these models talk about *keyframes* that are stored in full, and interpolation frames that are stored purely as derivation by moving and rotating *blocks* (to continue our cube analogy) of the video between one frame and the next. So you have a model that assumes coherence between one frame of video and the next, and might ignore small variations of color and intensity if a signal can be mostly represented by moving blocks around. And even these blocks are represented with an assumption of periodicity, an assumption that the color of one pixel is likely to be smoothly related to the color of its neighbors. So to stretch out a signal in this form means you're stretching vectors of motion rather than a mesh of colors, and if you have a video that fits these assumptions, for instance video of a runner sprinting across a track, when you stretch out the motion vectors you will really be slowing down the runner's motion and it will fit our expectations about slow motion instead of just fading one frame into the next, which is what happens when we stretch our original cube, so high-end video editing systems will use a vector-based representation as described for time-stretching«[1]

In *Montage Interdit*, Ochshorn explains, he was trying to match the size of the timeline of a video with the size of the video frame using timeline information inherited in the material like an index (HAIP 2012). In other words, he matches a graphical presentation of the length of a video with the size of a single frame. Representing each single frame of the video with just one selected pixel creates a slit-scan image of the video. Connecting the slit scan back to the video results in a timeline representation. At once the user can see what happens in a movie and has access to any point or any moment of a video without the tyranny of time. Without watching the whole video, the user is able to anticipate what seems to be essential. *Montage Interdit* in other words is a documentary archive annotated by an editor and combined with a zoom-based interface to allow users to look at the whole archive via an index of clips at once. Basically it is similar in operation to Google Earth.

Ochshorn's method of presenting and fast scanning a video matches observations of habits of people to click in the timelines of videos that are presented with control functions to adjust the video to its point of interest, and select only the playback stream for this point of interest—that is, the part of the video they want to watch. With growing amounts of audiovisual materials, Ochshorn's method of compression allows fast scanning of huge amounts in no time, which seems to be essential in handling and finding audiovisual materials of interest.

Ochshorn says that he also mapped a frame onto a previous frame, so the effect cascades. The video appears to be stabilized. The edges remain on screen and accessible. What has been before becomes accessible. The video becomes an advisory or announcement of capturing the impossibility of seeing everything without seeing the film (HAIP 2012).

In his further work, Ochshorn studied the idea of continuity while trying to make a documentary, which is also an archive. The idea embedded would be a film that never ends. The process of the film was mainly the process of organizing all the material of a documentary film and designing

---

1   Email exchange with Robert Ochshorn in 2013.

a user interface that can present it. The interface would allow users to switch between scholarly discussions and video clips. Users could add their own commentaries via an extended interface with a webcam. The resulting work is able to grow and change; it is transitional as it takes us from where we were to where we can be. Ochshorn's idea breaks with the tyranny of the canon, the specifications of genre, the modes of mass-produced media objects while simply defining them as interactive archives or databases open for a growing depth. The interface is the entrance. This could be applied to all kinds of cultural objects. As it is impossible to see all videos, read all books, or hear all songs, the single view and the single frame as interfaces are possible.

»My teenage years were concurrent with the first consumer-grade digital camcorders, and I spent a good chunk of my spare time making videos with my friends. YouTube wasn't launched until I finished high school, and my parents' dial-up Internet generally wasn't up to the demands of video anyway, so we released all of our creations on DVDs with elaborate menus, hidden features, etc. It was a decision made without much thought, a sort of "default." YouTube or Vimeo might have taken this place of a "default" for a while, but I believe for a variety of reasons that we're moving beyond that phase, and that the limitations of these generic web video distributors are being sharply felt.«[2]

In the near future these limitations will be overcome, and cultural or industrial temporal objects will be accessible in an archive database, where all movies are there at once by looking at a single one. Practices like Robert Ochshorn's will become normative and change the way we use and act with—what should we call it if it is not really a movie, not the single thing? Things.

In his 1999 book *In the Beginning Was the Command Line,* Neal Stephenson wrote:

»Now the first job that any coder needs to do when writing a new piece of software is to figure out how to take the information that is being worked with (in a

---

2   See: http://videovortex9.net/events_tags/robert-m-ochshorn/

graphics program, an image; in a spreadsheet, a grid of numbers) and turn it into a linear string of bytes. These strings of bytes are commonly called files or (somewhat more highly) streams. They are to telegrams what modern humans are to Cro-Magnon man, which is to say, the same thing under a different name. All that you see on your computer screen—your Tomb Raider, your digitized voice mail messages, faxes, and word-processing documents written in thirty-seven different typefaces—is still, from the computer's point of view, just like telegrams, except much longer and demanding of more arithmetic.« (Stephenson 1999, 15)

Simply put, a digital moving image or video is just more work for a computer and a much bigger set of data to process. Processing is the magic keyword. The methods of processing of data information creates the possibilities not only of extracting and interfacing with data in extraordinarily large sets, it also opens up a field of creative enterprise in breaking conventions as simple as the video clip. The clip seems to be a determined object, but is actually just another interface projecting possibilities of other worlds.

Max/Jitter

In the 1980s in Paris at the IRCAM, Miller Puckett developed a music composing software with a graphical user interface to be used with the Apple Macintosh computers. The software became a visual programming environment used not only by music composers, performers, and software designers, but also by visual artists to create interactive multimedia installations (Max [software] 2014). Miller Puckett named the software Max after one of the fathers of computer music, Max Matthews.

»MAX reuses the patchable modular analog synthesizer metaphor. You build patches by placing modules on a graphic surface and connecting these modules together with patch cords. The connections represent paths on which values or signal streams are send between the modules. These modules are either processing units (arithmetics, timing, ...), data containers (tables, ...), system inputs and outputs (audio, MIDI, ...). MAX modules are called objects in the sense of Object-Oriented Languages. Objects can themselves be patchers, so that a patch has a hierarchical structure. Some objects have graphical interactive behavior and can be used as controllers, to change values in the patch, or as viewers, to display values computed by the patch.« (jMax n.d.)

Max developed to *Max MSP* and later added *Jitter* as a video toolbox. *Jitter* was an extension of the software environment to create filters and effects for video, adjust color, distort images, or create video image and signal through manipulation of frequencies in various modules. Life videos can be combined with graphics, composited or filtered with other sources.

Each frame of video is handled and stored as a grid of color values. The same matrix can be used to store sounds, 3D geometry data, or any other kind of values that would fit in the grid. In processing the grid, the visual artist can fluidly move between various forms of media and translate them to his needs. Matrices make it possible to transcode information, take it from one kind and convert it to a different kind of output, shifting between video, sound, graphics, or even text.

»A matrix is most easily thought of as a grid, usually of two dimensions or more. (A one-dimensional array is what programmers call an array, which is basically just a list.) We'll start with 2D grids; think of a chessboard. The crucial elements of a grid are these:
1. each location (cell) in the grid contains information. 2. each location has a unique address.
Matrixes matter in Jitter, because the program stores the information about what is visible on your computer screen through matrixes. A screen is made up of a number of pixels, say 1024 x 768 = 786,432 individual cells or locations. And each of these pixels has a color that is determined by three values signfiying the precise mixture of red, blue and, green light on a scale of 0-255. Jitter, like Photoshop, stores a 4th piece of information which is the equivalent of Photoshop's alpha channel and is used similarly for masking and mixing effects (transparency/opacity).« (Video in MAX 2009)

Jitter, like a video synthesizer, is a tool that digitally creates a video signal. A video synthesizer originates from an analog instrument that creates signals electronically. Similar to a video synthesizer, *Jitter* is able to generate visual material without a camera input through the use of its various modules. In a video synthesizer, the various internal video pattern generators would generate the signal or a camera or signal input could be used to enhance or manipulate the electronic signal.

»The history of video synthesis is tied to a "real time performance" ethic. The equipment is usually expected to function on input camera signals the machine has never seen before, delivering a processed signal continuously and with a minimum of delay in response to the ever changing live video inputs. Following in the tradition of performance instruments of the audio synthesis world such as the Theremin, video synthesizers were designed with the expectation they would be played in live concert theatrical situations or set up in a studio ready to process a videotape from a playback VCR in real time while recording the results on a second VCR. Venues of these performances included "Electronic Visualization Events" in Chicago, The Kitchen in NYC, and museum installations. Video artist/performer Don Slepian [1] designed, built and performed a foot-controlled Visual Instrument at the Centre Pompideau in Paris (1983) and the NY Open Center that combined genlocked early micro-computers Apple II Plus with the Chromaton 14 Video Synthesizer [2] and channels of colorized video feedback.

Analog and early real time digital synthesizers existed before modern computer 3D modeling. Typical 3D renderers are not real time, as they concentrate on computing each frame from, for example, a recursive ray tracing algorithm, however long it takes. This distinguishes them from video synthesizers, which MUST deliver a new output frame by the time the last one has been shown, and repeat this performance continuously (typically delivering a new frame regularly every 1/30 or 1/25 of a second). The real time constraint results in a difference in design philosophy between these two classes of systems.« (Video synthesizer 2014)

Jitter is a tool for live performance as well as multimedia installations and visual effects. It is part of a cultural development where music and visuals or moving images combined are used in performances. A VJ operates a video synthesizing tool while a DJ mixes music in concert halls, clubs, or galleries. What is sometimes called "visual music" has its visual roots in music videos and experimental avant-garde films and its musical roots in avant-garde practices in the music and performance scenes worldwide. The video is processed live in real-time as the sound of the music is. Video performance tools work with data sets of basic loops, which can be called, looped, layered, manipulated, stretched, squeezed, and so on, similar to the performed music; together with the music, it creates the sensual stimulating audiovisual environment. Rhythm, lights, and colors are the basic principles of organizing a database of video generators, transitions, and filter modules as well as ready sets of video archives. The loop is the basic engine.

Another tool for understanding video as a process or accessing video in process is the software application *Processing*. Initially developed from a sketchbook software to teach computer-programming fundamentals, its widespread active user community developed *Processing* into a creative software tool for artists and researchers allowing them to write, edit, and compile applications running Java code (Processing n.d.).

Processing accommodates what Lev Manovich, in his 2001 book *The Language of New Media,* suggested that future filmmakers should learn programming. As a simple tool, Processing enables non-programmers to get started with programming while providing visual feedback. The impact or effect of the written code can immediately be demonstrated (Processing [programming language] 2014). »But the most important thing about Processing and culture is not high-profile results—it's how the software has engaged a new generation of visual artists to consider programming as an essential part of their creative practice.« (Processing n.d.)

A filmmaker might be at the same time a programmer, a visual artist, and a software developer, since what appears as a video clip is already transformed through digital cultural operations into an interface and object of transmedia, cross-cutting and intersecting various areas and organizational forms of cultural data. Software environments like *Processing* recall analog signal manipulations in combination with frame generation and filtering. Manovich describes these operations as characteristics of new media, analyzing the influence of software on cinema and vice versa. Years later, we are still distinguishing between these cultural forms, but are already experiencing our adaptation to such practices and the changes in daily life and everyday temporal objects.

EXTERIORS

As deeply as the interior of a video clip can be extracted, stretched, or dived into, so can a clip and/or its single frames be expanded with layers and code outside or on top of the temporal object. A simple way to expand a video is to add a layer on top of its representation, the container building its viewer object inside a website.

In its first seconds, the Vertical Video Syndrome PSA I mentioned earlier shows a John Goodman portrait layer. On the portrait is placed a normally invisible object, which, when the mouse moves over the portrait, suggests that users click for a link to another video of the Hollywood actor screaming. In some software, such objects are called sprites. These sprites represent when, where, and how something appears in a predefined area and related to a time in a clip. One of the multimedia developing tools of the past, *Macromedia Director* would use sprites to call cast members to appear on stage in a movie. *Movie, stage, cast* are all terminologies from the cinema and the theater adapted to develop multimedia applications. Brenda Laurel's book *Computers as Theatre* is one of the first scholarly works to apply aesthetics and dramatic structures and methodologies to thinking about computers or to solving problems posted by them and digital tool sets in a creative and experiential way. An interactive movie is a process of defining a stage and time when diverse objects appear, how they behave, and what their properties are. HTML5 in a similar way allows us to understand a video as an object that is not just embedded but has appearance, behaviors, and properties that can be customized according to the properties, events, behaviors, actions, and conditions created or anticipated through users and things. The video in HTML5 is not bound to a single viewer and a single screen. In the flat screen on the webpage, it can expand its visual borders and break standardizations to create affective experiences

The idea behind the development of HTML5 was as Sylvia Pfeiffer describes it the basic idea of a "Continuous Media Web" (Pfeiffer 2010, x). This web would compose all information out of audio and video content. Browsing through this web would be similar to browsing text and image based pages by following hyperlinks. Temporal objects would be linked to transcripts of their content allowing conventional indexing for deep searches inside media.

A Hunter _____ a Bear, or the Tipp-experience, is an interactive video advertisement on YouTube for the company TippEx, the biggest European producer of correction products (TippEX 2010). Launched in 2010, the video allows the user to »white and rewrite« the video's title in order to influence the story of the hunter, who does not want to shoot a bear. The user is asked to write what the hunter should do after he reached out of the frame, grabbed the TippEx whitening tool, and whitened the word "shoot" out. If the user now writes a verb like dance or anything else the hunter could do with the bear, another video of the hunter and the bear is loaded and it shows, for example, the two dancing. Various videos of variations of actions instead of shooting are available.

Illustration 6: The tippexperience

Source: http://www.youtube.com/watch?v=nZBzy0FzKuA [5.12.14]

»To the campaign's credit (perhaps because it's European), the options for what you can suggest the bear and hunter do together include some decidedly un-Puritan suggestions befitting YouTube's more adolescent users. Because yes, if you're a dirty-minded human being and you plug the obvious four-letter word into the box, the expected result occurs. (I'm not dirty-minded, okay? It was a journalistic imperative.) While it's more fun to discover potential suggestions yourself, the page is full of comments from happy users, and while it is possible to discover the limits of what the designers of the experience have created ("sambas with," "parties with," and "dances with" return the same result, for example) there's a surprising amount of variety at play. The Tipp-Experience launched officially at the beginning of September, but it's a testament to its evergreen quality that it feels fresh and fun even a month later. The technology is flawless, the design deceptively simple; it's almost easy to take this sort of thing for granted. Which makes one wonder—what will "wow" web audiences next?« (Miller 2010)

In the second installment of the Tipp-Experience in 2012, the producers developed the idea of a birthday party for the bear while a comet is crashing into the world. By again changing the title, the user can transport bear and hunter through history to a different year to continue the party. New funny videos with both characters in historical situations are loaded and played, creating the illusion of time travel.

»We received a massive worldwide PR coverage for the launching of the campaign (mashable, creativity online, Ad Age...). There were more than 250,000 shares on Facebook and up to one tweet per second on the campaign during the first 24 hours. More than one million people took part to the experience during the first day and the intro video has been ranked the second most viewed digital commercial in the world during the first week of the launching (viral video chart data), contributing to the massive worldwide success of the campaign. It also won two Bronze Lions in cyber category of the Cannes Advertising Festival.« (TippEx 2012)

But not only HTML5 opens up the browser screen: video could be layered or connected with data coming from sensors sensing the surrounding viewing environment or any remote environment in the real physical world. A simple example could be the combination with depth information collected from a Kinect sensor that registers any object and object change in front of the screen. The Kinect sensor consists of a camera and an infrared sensor attached to the actual recording camera. Another simpler possibility could be the combination with data filtered from an active camera. A viewer's gesture could control the play experience and therefore replace other elements on the screen. Environmental data, object data, and bio-data are all possible information that could be combined with the temporal experience of a video clip. They could control the appearance, behavior, and properties of the clip. We actually could step into a movie and walk around like Alice in Wonderland entering the phantasy world and meet marvelous companions and live a narrative. This is the reverse move of Woody Allen's *The Purple Rose of Cairo*, where we enter a movie world and are standing on a screen as actors of temporal phantasies.

An artist exploring the extension of video into the physical space is Camille Utterback, who won the MacArthur "genius" award in 2009. In her installation work *Text Rain*, Utterback combines the letters from the text of a poem projected as rain on a screen with live camera footage of spectators onto the same screen, so the letters rain on the spectators. The movement and gestures of the spectators are processed live and influence the falling of the letters.

Her *Liquid Time* series of interactive installations between 2000 and 2002 »explores how the concept of 'point of view' is predicated on embodied existence« (Utterback 2000-2002).

A visitor or participant's physical motion in the installation space creates a fragmentation in a projected video clip. »The fragmentation looks not only like the video is turning to liquid, but also like one is traveling back in time to an older period of the same scene« (Lee 2010). Moving closer to the projection results in a deeper move in time, while moving away heals the fragmented image. »The interface of one's body—which can only exist in one place, at one time—becomes the means to create a space in which multiple times and perspectives coexist. The resulting imagery can be described as video cubism« (Utterback 2000-2002).

Illustration 7: Camille Utterback – Liquid Time 2000-2002

Source: http://camilleutterback.com/projects/liquid-time-series/

Utterback chooses the video image as basic unit of playback. The frame is deconstructed. Similar to Ochshorn's approach, Utterback plays with the basic premises of temporal audiovisual objects or time-based media collapsing recording and playback. Time and space are disrupted by the user's presence, motion, and gesture.

»The current Liquid Time Series consists of two distinct pieces, Liquid Time—Tokyo, and Liquid Time—New York. In each piece, participants interact with images from sites in these cities where humans, data, or other physical matter are transferred or in transit. Participants' movement back and forth in front of the screen both echoes and controls the movements of busy pedestrians. People on screen are set in motion by motions off screen—shimmering in and out of existence. The composition in each video clip is anchored by static elements that become stable armatures in the chaos of fragmentation—street signs, trash cans, a person standing oddly still. The unexpected permanence of certain elements (and the transience of others) hint at how both personal and cultural memory have a physical component subject to the unpredictable nature of decay.« (Utterback 2000-2002)

SPACE IS ONLY NOISE[1]

> The creation of the world was the first sabotage. Why so, Cioran once asked? Because its creation destroyed the possibility of all other worlds which could be made on this particular planet.
> BAXTER PHILLIPS (1988)

> Das Internet lässt zum Beispiel... Minutenfilme zu. Das war der Anfang der Filmkunst. 1902 gibt es überhaupt nur Minutenfilme. Und wenn Sie diese Form haben, die übrigens der Kamera sehr entspricht, das sie einen Momenteindruck zu einem Film machen, nicht aufblasen, keine Dramaturgie brauchen, dann können Sie daraus Konstellationen machen, und die können 10 Stunden lang werden. Und jetzt haben sie einerseits den Zusammenhang, Kontext, und andererseits Moment, also die zwei Elemente, und so geht die Filmgeschichte in meinen Augen weiter.
> ALEXANDER KLUGE[2]

---

1 The title of this chapter refers to a song by Nicholas Jaar called *Space Is Only Noise If You Can See*. This song was used in the trailer for one of the latest works by Blast Theory called *I'd Hide You* presented at Sheffield Docfest in 2013. http://www.blasttheory.co.uk/projects/id-hide-you/

FIRST SABOTAGE[3]

The Romanian-born philosopher and essayist E.M. Cioran wrote this simple sentence »The creation was the first sabotage.« in his 1952 book *All Gall Is Divided*. It is a straightforward definition, an aphorism making a clear statement: Our world could have been different.

»'That there should be a reality hidden by appearances is, after all, quite possible; that language might render such a thing would be an absurd hope'—and nurses an ongoing fascination with the possibilities death holds for release from life's madness. (When the Dead Kennedys sang, 'I look forward to death / This world brings me down,' they might as well have been taking notes from Cioran.).« (Cioran 1952)

Cioran seems to be a deep pessimist, someone who is more in favor and convinced by his personal reflections than by abstract thought. »I've invented nothing; I've simply been the secretary of my sensations« (Emil Cioran 2013).

Cioran's aphorism about the »creation« is a discovery through another text, the introduction of a little-known source on censorship, sex, and violence in Hollywood: Baxter Phillips's 1975 book *Cut: The Unseen Cinema*, which tells the story of Hollywood movies censored because of their violent or sexual content from the beginnings of cinema up to the 1970s. In his introduction, he continues his discussion of Cioran's aphorism:

»The creation of a film is also a sabotage. It prevents another film being made on the same subject; it uses up on its budget the money, which could have made other

---

2 Die kleine Filmfabrik (2012). »The Internet allows for example ... minute movies. That was the beginning of the film art. In 1902 there were only minute movies. And if you have this form, which corresponds very much the camera, that you make an instant impression into a film, not inflate, don't need drama, then you can create constellations, which can be 10 hours long. And now you have on one hand the context, and on the other hand the moment, so the two elements. And so the film history continues in my eyes.« (My translation.)

3 The following chapter builds on a talk I gave at Amber Platform, Istanbul in November 2013.

films; it is completed in a form, which is often unsatisfactory to financier, director, distributor and audience. The final print of a film is its first censorship, because it eliminates all other possible versions of that film at that time. As the old Hollywood saying goes, the only positive thing about a film is a negative. In the laboratories lies the unkindest cut of all, the last chance.« (Philips 1988, 7)

We always seem to take a film in cinema for granted. We never consider that there have been decisions made that stopped other ideas from being realized. We never consider that a dictatorship of a single narrative, of one single directive, is on display and taking place. Somebody forced one single ultimate narrative out, eliminating all possible others or streamlining all elements in a single entity. Like cinema, we are taking the one world we are living in for granted.

THE MOST IMPORTANT IMAGE

»In 1996, scientists took a huge risk when they pointed the Hubble telescope to an inky field that they believed to be void of stars and planets. As images from Hubble are in constant demand, the worry was that devoting so much time to a black space would prove futile. Once the photons finally registered, though, that leap of faith proved fruitful: light from over three thousand galaxies illuminated the image. A few years and missions later, Hubble's glimpse into what is known as the deep field has revealed that we are just one tiny part of a vast system comprising 100 billion galaxies.« (Cox 2013)

All of a sudden there is a space deeper than we imagined. The system we were living in or with was already a vast system and hard to imagine, but these images revealed a much deeper complexity.

A simple field in the vision of a space-based telescope opens up a new window to another enormous landscape of galaxies. It was a marvelous but scary look. Most important than the look out, with this window information hits us at a speed faster than light, something that for any living human being is unimaginable since nothing is supposed to be faster than light itself. Einstein's Theory of Relativity states that the speed of light is the maximum speed. But it is simply true and we learn the reason, a simple proof of a movement—while the information moves toward us, the universe is expanding. More distant galaxies seem to be moving away from us even faster than closer galaxies. It is possible that they could move faster than light. In this case, light from these galaxies will never reach us. When their light reaches us, they will already be gone (Cain 2008).[4]

I want to come back to the image Hubble sent, the image of a vast system of galaxies far, far in deep space. On a two-dimensional plane, a photographic reproduction of all these millions of dots appears as visual noise, a kind of televised snow, a random dot pattern, like the static we might remember from analog video or television.

NOISE, FACEBOOK FACES, AND THE VIDEOSPHERE

We are looking at a space. The space is present as this random dot pattern.

Another similar random dot pattern appears in media artist Natalia Rojas's project *The Faces of Facebook*. The pattern is the presentation of 1,278,842,363 Facebook profile pictures in a single web page.

»Because there we are, all mixed up: large families, women wearing burkas, many Leo Messis, people supporting same-sex marriages of r4bia, Chihuahuas, Indian Gods, tourists pushing the leaning Tower of Pisa, selfies, nowborns, Ferraris, studio black and white portraits, a lot of weddings but zero divorces, ID photos, faces framed in hearts, best friends, manga characters, politic logos, deep looks, love messages, eyes, memes, smiles, sweet grandparents and some not-yet-censured pictures.« (Rojas n.d.)

Moving the mouse over the noisy image reveals numbers of Facebook faces; a click zooms in and a range of neighboring Facebook profiles appears. There is a chance that you'll find your own profile picture. It's interesting that the collage of the squares, an assemblage of personal instances, profiles somehow fits the suggested color spectrum of the 14x8 square on my screen. It's interesting that the software first zooms to an amount of colored square placeholders or keyframes and then fills them with the individual

---

4   On faster-than-light travel, see Faster-than-light (2014), which gives a much more detailed insight of what could be possible or imaginable scientifically.

profile pictures, setting them into boxes, cartographical coordinates, fixed entities in a seemingly not-so-fixed world. Each profile has been given a location in the noise. The image of noise is just a map we are looking at from far, far away. In the case of this application, it is a static map.

What would happen if each of these profile images and dots in the noise pattern were dynamic, in a kind of flux or constant flow. Of course, the profile pictures here in this application are still changed from time to time by their users or owners, but this still guarantees a static representation. If each element were to change constantly in itself, that means it would be moving, then they would all be much like video. The application would be a vertical cut inside a video sphere creating a two-dimensional plane, a flat surface of changing images. There would be multiple instances and multiple possible planes, or multiple screens. Each of them would be related to a specific moment on a linear timescale, but would suggest that at the same time and in the same presence there are multiple moments on the intersecting scales or lines. In this manner, multiple video worlds or video spheres exist.

All these multiple changing items, elements, or objects are temporally coming into being and are radically available to us. Objects are embedded in an environment (*Umwelt*) and affect each other; they are inseparable from the space surrounding them, and the space is inseparable from the elements embedded. An environment can be »inhabited by for example video-enabled devices and objects that we either touch or that touch us in our physical space« (Treske 2013)

Environments or spheres, both atmospheric temporary constructions, can take the form of hybrid spaces, crossing over from the virtual of the net to the tangible of the physical into the so-called real—that site of power, history, memory and stability in form of the city square.

The Facebook application does not zoom in on the individual profile pictures; it obviously tries to keep a distance and therefore maintain the privacy of the individual. Instead, we have to overcome and enter the privacy by other means or by just simply being a part of the same shared environment or space, in this case being a friend in Facebook.

The Hubble images lack closeness and detail, maintaining a distance. Even as the image comes to us, it is distant to the depicted, scanned objects; they are strangers and stay strangely unidentified. A moment later the distance has grown.

But we might read this information much differently. We are aware of the distance and we relate to the atmosphere of it more closely and naturally than to the possibility of having another object, a world similar to ours, which know cannot be. It is certain, just from viewing all the recorded videos as modes of seeing surrounding us are projecting, that our relationship with the world as our environment has dramatically changed. When we move through physical space and through virtual space, we employ tactics and strategies to create our own strings and trajectories in theses spaces. It is important to recognize that we are not the ones defining these spaces; rather, they are defined by others and private in their means. The strings, trajectories, and flows of our movements are mirrors of our subjectivity and determined by our interaction with the society we are living in (Treske 2013).

Our relation to the world is, as Villem Flusser had pointed out, already more experimental. We are experiencing and operating with potentialities of our world and other worlds. It is therefore easy just to build and experiment with what is surrounding us on a trial and error basis.

Flusser notes: »Indeed we are actively generating our tools and through them we are generating the world, but it is also true that those tools are hitting back on us and are generating us« (Zielinski 2014).

Sitting behind the keyboard or looking at a device in our hand opens up the view on an infinite »swarm of particles« changeable by a simple operation anytime. The way we experience the world is already an imagination of a digital code, a world that is projected through binaries. Governments and actual power in physical space as well as their instruments are still projecting a world that is already in decline. According to Flusser, a war in dimensions is going on as we are moving to the zero dimension.

Flusser defined the zero dimension as the dimension of pure numbers and algorithm in his anthropology of cultural techniques. According to him, 4D would be spatial/temporal orientation in the real world of moving things/objects; 3D is architecture, sculpture, monuments, artifacts; 2D is image; and 1D is linear text, writing with the alphanumeric code. All of these dimensions have existed at the same time throughout history but with different weights and directions. »For Flusser this 0-dimension is a passage for building up a relationship or an attitude towards the world in which an important shift of paradigms takes place: from subjectivity to projectivity« (Zielinski 2014).

In the video sphere a single video is a relational item, an element of a temporal spatial relation described as a video. The idea of the video sphere and Flusser's 0-dimension come together in the understanding of a passage for building an attitude toward the world. This world is a world of projectivity, a world of constructive action, constantly reshaping and changing. A video temporarily opens a window toward an understanding of the world through its view, its invitation to look at, its atmosphere of sharing. It can easily be reshaped or remixed. It is authored in the process and cannot be owned. The original source of the element is not necessary, as it is always available and accessible in multiple forms.

Procedural content creation—building worlds, breaking and placing blocks—seems to be the objective of the game *Minecraft*, but this might not be the main reason why a relatively simple or primitive game is as popular as this one is. Wandering around, following location-based scouting activities, searching for perfect cliffs and perfect sunsets—this still does not give a real explanation for the fascination with *Minecraft*. But what the game simulates has lots to do with the way we would like to experience our world, would like to learn about creating things, following processes of construction.

Minecraft was developed independently and is now one of the most successful computer games. It uses very simple pixelated graphics and block-like elements. As a game, it has no real direction or specific guidelines. No plot guides the player or gives tasks.

»'The pixelated style might appear simple but it masks a huge amount of depth and complexity,' explains Alex Wiltshire, former editor of Edge magazine and author of forthcoming Minecraft guide, Block-o-pedia. 'Its complex nature doesn't lie in detailed art assets, but in how each element of the game interrelates.'« (Costello 2014)

At the beginning of the game, the novice player can choose between two modes of play: creation or survival. The central focus is in crafting tools and collecting resources to build whatever we want. Jane Costello describes in the *Guardian* her first playing experience together with her son Otis. Not knowing what to do when thrown onto an island in the creation mode, she was wandering around looking for things to do. Her son suggested and showed her how to build a roller coaster, something she wouldn't have thought about. The creative mode provides unrestricted access to building blocks and tools, the ability not only to walk and swim, but also to fly and see the built structures from various views.

The survival mode is tough on its players. Monsters, zombies, and other kinds of pixelated creatures appear, destroying whatever they find and coming after the player's avatar. The player needs to build structures to protect himself.

»Whether it's crafting more powerful weapons to fend off creatures of the night or building that mega fortress to mock other miners in the open world, you're still going to need the precise raw materials. Make no mistake: this game is a grinder. But after toiling for hours and hours, finally stumbling upon that precious material you need is a priceless moment in its own right.« (Cho 2013)

Minecraft is very addictive and therefore very time consuming. It is also very imaginative and allows a huge amount of personal freedom in play. It can be used as a learning tool as it involves problem solving, imagination, memory, creativity, and logical sequencing. The game is not gender specific and involves very little violence, with the exception of fighting the zombies. *Minecraft* can also be used for filmmaking with its built-in procedural content creation engine to create landscapes or infinite universes (Hancock 2014).

ONLINE VIDEO, DOMESTIC BIRDS AND POLITICS

A single web video comes to my mind—a long hall filled with hundreds or thousands of domestic turkeys. A man in white hygienic clothing with mask and hair cover is giving a speech to the birds. The setting resembles a political talk. In each pause, the birds answer, applauding. The man emphasizes with his gestures the intended impression. The man calls out:

> "Eh ahali, (Well folks)
> (Pause and Birds answer)
> Sizin icin burdayim, (I am here for you)
> (Pause and Birds answer)
> ….

In May 2013 YouTube user *Pelin S.* shared the video as the funniest video of the year. In 2010 it was already once the funniest video of the year in Turkey.[5] The video invites and animates us to laugh. The man talking to the birds seems like a fool giving a talk to animals, but ironically impersonates a politician talking to the population. The recorded speech and its main character remind us of characters like Nasrettin Hoca or Eulenspiegel, a fool, clown, harlequin, a trickster, whose tricks are a sabotage of our world. Irony builds a »contrast, between what the expectations of a situation are and what is really the case« (Irony 2014).

As I have tried to show, in a world or universe that appears as noise, how can we find a video like this? How can the video of the speech to the birds reach us and get our attention? Such a video is not necessary programmed on one of the national television or broadcast stations. It is somewhere in the realm of the web. All of a sudden, at any time, it is shared and referred to. When the video appears, it attracts us. This is the same in 2013 as it was in 2010. The context of the video in 2013 is rather different than the context I created in 2010 in my installation. The motivation for sharing was similar. The web creates a radical availability of anytime and anywhere.

To become aware of this video, we just need to be in a shared and networked environment at anytime and anyplace.

»*Anyness* still commonly serves as the guiding principle of freedom, achievement, and attainment that drives Internet design. *Any* music, text, video, available any-

---

5   In January 2015 the video is no longer available on YouTube (http://www.youtube.com/watch?v=MIUwbg-8Ep8). The video is in my personal archive as I had used it in 2010 for an interactive video installation.

The installation „Videocu" invited visitors in a shop setting during Ankara Film Festival 2010 to select, view, and enjoy the most popular online videos shared between people from Ankara and their worldwide friends in January and February 2010 on YouTube and Facebook.

The above video was its opening video. Whenever the system rebooted it would start with this video as a speech to the public. The context of the "Videocu" installation was of course the change in media and media forms, the disappearance of video and its architecture the video rental store through online video.

where, anytime. Tablets and smartphones have fluid uses, turning into *any* device that can be accommodated by the fixed physical attributes. A tablet might be a book, a guitar tuner, sketchpad, and so on. Gradually, even the physical properties of gadgets will become more mutable.« (Lanier 2010, 392)

BREAK -------------------------- JUNE 1ST, 2013

On June 1, 2013 the television channels were still silent. There was no news broadcasted about the gatherings on the streets in Istanbul, Ankara, or Izmir. There was no news broadcasted about the violent gas attacks of riot police in the city centers. Images and videos of the events at night were running through Facebook and Twitter. At night a Norwegian TV station had a live broadcast bought from a Turkish agency (DHA) from behind a police truck. A small Turkish television channel supporting the opposition party in parliament picked up the news of the event, but the main media outlets stayed silent for the night and the following day.

In the morning of June 1, people started to walk over one of the Istanbul bridges from Asia to Europe to join in the protests at Taksim Square. Very early after the first news of the march, a photo appeared on Facebook showing a huge group of demonstrators on the bridge. The photograph was a long shot taken from far away from the bridge. Later during the day other photos appeared in social media outlets and were shared mainly on Facebook and Twitter showing masses of demonstrators walking over the bridge. Were these photos real? Were they manipulated with Photoshop?

When the first news arrived, somebody ("a friend") drove with his car from the European to the Anatolian side of Istanbul, and while passing the walking people he recorded a video on his mobile phone.

The event was suddenly real. It was many people, not as many as the images on Facebook had suggested, but enough to support the ideas shared.

Following the events in the next hours, videos shared over the web not only supported the authenticity of images and short tweets of people involved or observing. The shared videos took over the space television had left empty. These videos created a ground zero feeling. They created togetherness with the demonstrators, spreading the event much faster and wider over the country.

Illustration 8: Istanbul Bosporus Bridge on the 2nd day of Gezi

Source: Unknown (Facebook June 2013).

THE VIDEOS OF #GEZIPARK

The videos were clearly in relation with tweets shared before or at the same time in the same group of followers, multiplying each single instant immediately. It had built a network, mapping an event and following its progress. The videos appeared amateurish at first, immediate snapshots shaped by circumstances. Soon they were followed by edits with underlying music.

These edits or short assemblages of event-related sequences of moving images were more in the style of music videos, emphasizing an overall feeling and mood of togetherness and freedom with resistance and occupation. The atmosphere of these videos was not necessary political in the sense of an organized producing body, but rather was comparable with the average mash of YouTube footage. Yet, as such, these online videos documented a new form of media literacy grounded in Turkish and international youth subculture.

In this situation, conventional forms of media or *temporal objects* as produced by the *programming industries* (Bernard Stiegler)—meaning television—disappeared.

The programming industries did not act or react to the events. In their absence, the videos streamed or shared online did not take any preexisting form or genre for granted. They became spontaneous expressions of feelings and feelings of solidarity. They did not aim to be flawless, well-organized representations matching aesthetic criteria. They were mainly internal referenced. Some of these videos might not even be understandable outside of the event or apart from the participants in both spaces—real and virtual.

The silence of the programming industries is very telling in the sense that it can be interpreted not only politically but also culturally as a break in transmission, a holdup in the flow of *temporal objects*, and then in the interruption of *servicing* consciousness (as Andrew Clay formulated it in an email exchange is). The web and mobile video enter as noise, static, glitch, over the TV signal that is ignoring the event. In more general terms, the TV transmission is unable to spatialize life in the same way as web and mobile video.

But, of course, what appears as videos of the event might be lost or appear as noise overall, and if you do not zoom in, the noise is all you see.

VIDEO STYLE AND VIDEO ACTIVISM

It is obvious that there is a close relation in the applied aesthetical style of a range of the shared videos to what Ken Dancyger once named the *MTV Style* in his *Technique of Film and Video Editing*. Rooted in experimental filmmaking and the TV commercial, the MTV Style establishes its own reference points between reality and video time. The new correlation is provided by the vividness of the resulting imagery. The videos are a simulation of freedom and at the same time a rejection of traditions as well as the traditions of narrative. Time and place are anytime. They temporally and spatially dwell in anytime-whatever. These videos strategically prioritize defining and expressing an emotional atmospheric state.

In the videos of Gezi Park, the style is native to the users. Therefore they *see*. The videos have been part of a sphere, a space of flows and streams, which creates bubbles and foams, an environmental object related to a hybrid space of a social event or action with a common ground outside the private broadcasting industries. These videos are not »activist videos« in a traditional sense. They are not aimed to build a form of narrative. An activist video would follow a kind of predefined narrative subtext. In the context of Gezi, this type would be clear videos like REDHACK has produced and shared during the main events. The rhetoric of such videos shared during Gezi emphasizes social relations surrounding the video or videos. Similarities can be found in the youth protests in Greece or in Hong Kong in 2012.

»Through video is it possible to engage socially, even while not being there in the square, in the flesh. ... It's about being with someone via mediation, not despite mediation. The question of being there in the skin is simply a bit old fashioned. You can be there and engage without physical presence, through the enveloping sphere of video.« (Coleman 2013)

BATTLEFIELD V

Battlefield V - Taksim Direnişi 'GamePlay is a video published on Vimeo at the time of the Gezi protests. The title of the video suggests its relation and its perception. There is a clear reference toward the play of a first-person shooter game. The content description under the video is as follows:

»Forefront of Taksim resistance through the eyes of the rebel! Tear gas in the streets of Taksim. Struggle 'level' jumping. A brief summary from the perspective of the insurgents. The aim of the resistance is protection from the police. I is already evident in the video that the aim is not to attack the police. None of the shots in the video are mine, all recorded by others!" (Battlefield 5 2013)[6]

The video turns the real event into a game. It emphasizes the setting, the goal, and its continued repetition of similar actions to step up level by level. Ironically, the world depicted is not taken for granted but playfully described with its absurdness. The video and the game define a first-person space and a first-person subjective action projected on the event and shared between the participants in the overall hybrid sphere. Of course, the video addresses users who are familiar with the angles, perspectives, and actions of this kind of moving image mapped inside real Istanbul. The game play projects Istanbul and Taksim as a post-television geography. *Battlefield V* relates to a navigational space and shows the penetration of this space through its assembled camera footage. As Friedrich Kittler has discussed in

---

6   Translation from Turkish is mine.

the context of media technology, the video refers to a certain type of speech for certain types of people. This type of people unites with other types of people all mapped on the same space—an obvious, uncanny, chaotic, overpopulated social space like Istanbul. Public space converted to owned private space through means of power resulting in disorientation is remapped as a new kind of cultural space, which is customized and personalized for each person. In the past, television and radio have ordered events and produced a mass consciousness.

»The programming industries, and more specifically the mediatic industry of radio-televisual information, mass-produce temporal objects heard or seen simultaneously by millions of 'consciousness': this massive temporal co-incidence orders the event's new structure, to which new forms of consciousness and collective unconsciousness correspond.« (Steigler 2010)

Online videos shared on Facebook or Twitter appear in the relation of the event as space-medium. The protesters and the police are mapped onto a defined space. The space is not separable from the events, the people, and the videos. The space is shared between the real city squares and the squares of the screens connected online. It is repurposed and redescribed over and over again. It has become a living space in the process of change. As the programming industries are continuing to look for an ordered event and an "organization» or an body of formation, the web or online related hybrid event operates rather like a living entity, bearing a momentum of existence, which is rather nomadic, uncontrolled, and unshaped, and bearing similarity to an amoeba.

»Everything around you is all made up.
You are a person on a phone." (Blast Theory 2012)

The space of Gezi park, the space of Taksim, have become poetic spaces. They are no longer narrative. Through video-enabled mobile phones, digital video recording techniques, and social media sharing services, video proves to be a temporal space-making technology. Its foolish use by the users under constant surveillance proves a counter-sabotage to which the established culture and the established televised geography have only a limited operational and navigational manual. Its foolish use simply generates noise and glitches.

The question of authorship and responsibility has become secondary as the material of the assemblage already exists in various forms. The assemblage called "Battlefield V" is just one possibility of many other possibilities or multiplicities. The traditional set of political conflict is rendered meaningless. The video itself is just temporal evidence of production of time in a certain space. This is not the work of an artist, as the idea of artist in this context is already an unreal element of the past. As Flusser stated, »The artist is somebody who does something to be exhibited in public, and the same goes for the politician.« The artist and the politician impose an idea. Their act is a sabotage act on a space we are together continuing to dream, knowing that we are dreaming this space. »Future is realizing yourself, whereas past is having become unreal« (Flusser 1995).

»In the first volume of his epic novel, The Man without Qualities, Robert Musil wrote at the beginning of Chapter 4: "To get through open doors successfully, it is necessary to respect the fact that they have solid frames. This principle, by which the old professor had always lived, is simply a requisite of the sense of reality. However, if there is a sense of reality – and no one doubts its justification for existing – then there must also be something we might call a sense of possibility. Whoever has it, does not say, for example, this or that has happened, will happen, or must happen here; instead, they invent: this or that might, could, or ought to happen in this case. If they are told that something is the way it is, they think: Well, it could just as well be otherwise. Thus, the sense of possibility can be defined as the ability to conceive of everything there might be just as well and to attach no more importance to what is than to what is not.« (Flusser 1995)

OCEAN BLUE

»The object of contemporary economy is linked to the question of how memory can be constructed; how one's attention can be steered towards the ability to be able to characterize one's wishes, beliefs and sensations or to perceive their effects by dissolving flows and reassembling new ones. The public is the true customer of this economy. How to resist and create new worlds with a camera that is integrated in the flows (of cyberspace)?« (Lazzarato 2007, 2.7)

With all the video created with all the cameras around, constantly uploading, sharing, linking, and relating, an ocean of blue is covering our planet, an ocean of video. Resistance, as Lazzarato suggested several years ago when video was in another state, has become a matter of a playful awareness, collecting bricks, resources, and tools, to build structures to hide and defend, and later on to together develop stronger economies of things. Somehow the fight for the Internet is a fight to limit the expansion of free space. It is also a fight for the rejection of dominating narratives and narrative forms. Video turns to the clip as a resource to build with.

What might look from the far outside as noise and dust, might embed beautiful and fascinating living vistas of moving images, constantly changing, rearranging, assembling, evolving, collapsing, but never disappearing. Forms trap the planet as stylishly as Booka Shade's video *Crossing Borders*. Of course, this is only visual and seeable if its existence is accepted. It might be a texture, a skin, a surrounding sphere. These are all images, or metaphors trying to describe these objects, their forms, their behaviors and properties—objects formerly named video.

»Each particle of dust carries with it a unique vision of matter, movement, collectivity, interaction, affect, differentiation, composition and infinite darkness« (Negarestani 2008). And as Jussi Parikka notes: »There is something poetic about dust. It is the stuff of fairy tales, stories of deserted places; of attics and dunes, of places from so long ago they seem to have never existed. Dusty books—the time of the archive that layers slowly on shelves and manuscripts« (Parikka 2013).

What we might see from the outside, to continue in this metaphor, is compressed in various ways and is material to be built on and to compress further. Compression, following Ochshorn, requires us to make assumptions to limit the space of all the possibilities. The result of a total compression would just be noise. If something were no longer compressible then it would lack any pattern; it would contain nothing to find and rearrange. But if there are patterns visible and they can be filtered, then with the knowledge of the assumptions—nothing more than the ciphers, the codebooks—we can return the original builds. The patterns are creating the reality, a reality of how we live in our world.

In *The Pattern in the Stone*, Danny Hills wrote, »Whenever I design a chip the first thing I want to do is look at it under a microscope—not because I think I can learn something new by looking at it but because I am always fascinated by how a pattern can create reality« (Hills 2000).

Of course, all the videos online, created and shared, are just physically stored somewhere on hard disk and physical storage spaces, but recalling a software application like Google Earth simulating the map of our planet, we have access to these videos that have geotags, which identify location with time and space. The stamp creates a memory space layer on top of the map layer, the satellite image, the street view; embedded in the actual reality of place and movement is the same place with a different movement from a parallel existing continuum. This might have been past, but it is present as the street view is present right now and as I can just now scroll, wipe, and zoom through the software.

As Lev Manovich points out, »the 'properties' of digital media (how it can be edited, shared, and analyzed) are now defined by the particular software as opposed to solely being contained in the actual content (i.e., digital files)« (Manovich 2012).

The ways we access, author, and edit media have changed radically. To say that this is just because we are using computers and all materials in use are digital is simplistic: it fails to describe distribution, analysis, generation, and manipulation or processing through and from software. The way we experience media forms is the result of choices filtered for us by other individuals or private profit-oriented companies.

»In summary: the techniques, the tools, and the conventions of media software applications are not the result of a technological change from 'analog' to 'digital' media. The shift to digital enables the development of media authoring software—but it does not constrain the directions in which it already evolved and continues to evolve. They are the result of intellectual ideas by people who conceived of it in the first place (Ivan Sutherland, Douglass Engelbart, Alan Kay, etc.), the actual products created by software companies and open source communities, the cultural and social processes set up when many people and companies start using it, and software market forces and constraints.« (Manovich 2012)

Software controls how things appear, how something is seen. Software defines the properties of any object, its borders, its appearances, and its behaviors.

The Window

The history of film theory starts with the reflection of the window. The screen appears as an opening to another world constructed by the projected moving image. From early cinema and early film theory to video, the computer and software have come a long way, with various approaches and methodologies applied to describe and understand what happens with the moving images we are creating and us. By visualizing all videos of now together lined up, the resulting image might resemble an image we are already familiar with. As data is expanding exponentially and becoming such an incredible amount that a single human being never be able to make meaningful associations of even nano-scale amounts, automatic and algorithmic visualization tools (like the ones Manovich is researching and applying) create a compression or extraction of an understandable or meaningful chunk, resembling of course another common standardized or stereotyped image.

In 2007, the south transept glass window of the Cologne Cathedral was inaugurated. The window was designed by the German artist Gerhard Richter and had an enthusiastic reception. Richter had used small squares to create what appears to be a kind of modern pixelated image of colors and light shining through. Initially Richter had followed the request to create a figurative motif for the window, but then by coincidence discovered his much earlier color field paintings might be a much more honest possibility for the design.

»There was more to it than meaning-resistant abstraction. The interplay of light and color in the stained glass window also attracted Richter for its possibilities of new experience on old terrain. 'The main problem of my painting is the light,' he wrote back in 1964/65, by which he meant not the light of Impressionist plein-air painting but the instantaneous light of the photography that so often forms the basis for his paintings. From the early photos of family and friends to the sea and landscapes and the Baader-Meinhof cycle, light-generated photographs—preferably blurred and in the shades between grey and white—have provided the inspiration for Gerhard Richter's paintings. Only in the series of monochrome panels and the abstract works does light play no active role (here it is a matter of illumination rather than exposure). A stained-glass window, where the glass changes its coloration with the quality of the daylight, offers a new facet of this old theme that is the central issue.« (Kipphoff 2007)

Illustration 9: Window by Gerhard Richter, Cologne Cathedral

Source: Jv74 – Fotolia.com

Richter used an aleatoric computer program to design the windows, meaning some elements were left to chance. He selected 72 colors from the spectrum of traditional glass painting and created 11,263 glass squares for the 19 meter high and 106 square meter window. Three of the six lancet windows are rendered with the software; the three others are mirrored versions of the renders. Richter's work follows his studies on proportion, methods of random arrangement, mirroring and color matching. The design is also based on his 1974 painting *4096 Colors*.

»Within the whole of the picture, however, he works with the reflections of color areas. In this way there emerges at first the impression of complete arbitrariness in the distribution of color areas, until one notices in the small details that things correspond inversely and repeat themselves. Then one senses a hidden order behind the supposed chaos of elements and forms. This order is sensed rather than recognized. No sooner does the viewer believe himself to have discerned the principle than it again slips away. Richter contrives to combine chance and calculation.«[7]

---

7   See: http://www.goethe.de/kue/bku/kuw/en2577503.htm

Richter's work rejects an obvious meaning or message. He seems to neutralize the sacralized representative space of the church and provides an experience of lights and colors not transformed by the dominating narrative of the medieval space. Through the change of light Richter's work gains a state of permanent uninfluenced change.

»So it is the very place itself, and its changing light, that makes this window into a paradigmatic work of art of the late twentieth century. Unlike the earlier pictorial narratives, figurative representations or decorative patterns, which each fitted into its respective frame, Richter's illuminated abstraction is not determined by lancet and rosette. So, just as he turns his back on narrative, with this design he also transgresses the prescribed frame, where necessary at the edges simply cutting the glass squares. Richter gaily ignores the constrictions of his stained-glass windows. And breaks the bounds once again, by outshining them: "Let there be light" (Genesis 1:3).« (Kipphoff 2007)

ILLUSTRATIONS

Illustration 1: Şeker Ahmet. Woodcutter in the Forest.   28
Illustration 2: Radial image plot of Instagram uploads   64
Illustration 3: Erdal İnci. Camondo Stairs.   110
Illustration 4: Dan Oki. Generatio Aequivoca   114
Illustration 5: Adam Magyar. Stainless.   128
Illustration 6: The tippexperience   163
Illustration 7: Camille Utterback. Liquid Time Series   165
Illustration 8: Istanbul Bosporus Bridge on the 2nd day of Gezi   177
Illustration 9: Window by Gerhard Richter, Cologne Cathedral   185

BIBLIOGRAPHY

Agamben, Giorgio. 2006. *History and Infancy: On the Destruction of Experience* (trans. Liz Heron). London: Verso.

Aguilar, Mario. 2014. Behind the scenes of a crazy drone video shoot. *Gizmodo* [online]. 23 March. Available from: http://gizmodo.com/behind-the-scenes-of-a-crazy-drone-video-shoot-1549806243 [9 January 2015]

Allen, Greg. 2012. When people die, they sing songs: Chris Marker's *Stopover In Dubai* [online]. 31 July. Available from: http://greg.org/archive/2012/07/31/when_people_die_they_sing_songs_chris_markers_stopover_in_dubai.html [9 January 2015].

Allocca, Kevin. 2011. Why videos go viral. TED talk. [Video file]. Available from: http://www.ted.com/talks/kevin_allocca_why_videos_go_viral [4.12.2014

AMC Theaters allegedly calls FBI to interrogate a Google Glass wearer. *Slashdot* [online]. 21 January. Available from: http://yro.slashdot.org/story/14/01/21/0215214/amc-theaters-allegedly-calls-fbi-to-interrogate-a-google-glass-wearer [10 January 2015]

Anderson, Chris. 2010. How web video powers innovation (transcript). [Online]. September 2010. Available from: http://www.ted.com/talks/chris_anderson_how_web_video_powers_global_innovation/transcript [12 February 2014]

Anderson, Ricky II. 2013. 5 best GoPro videos on the web that aren't action sports. *Videomaker* [online]. 24 September. Available from. http://www.videomaker.com/videonews/2013/09/5-best-gopro-videos-on-the-web-that-arent-action-sports [10 January 2015]

Arbesman, Samuel. 2013. Let's bring the polymath — and the dabblers. *Wired* [online]. 13 December. Available from: http://www.wired.com/opinion/2013/12/165191/?cid=co15772704 [10 January 2014].

Arian, Arman. 2013. Citizen Worm (video). [Online]. Available from: http://www.youtube.com/watch?v=co1sjfX4yII [24 November 2014]

Arnheim, Rudolf. 1936. *Radio* (trans. Margaret Ludwig & Herbert Read). London: Faber.

Arnheim, Rudolf. 1957. *Film as Art*. Berkeley: University of California Press.

Association for Psychological Science. 2012. Repeated exposure to media images of traumatic events may be harmful to mental and physical health. *Psychological Science* [online]. 4 September. Available from: http://www.psychologicalscience.org/index.php/news/releases/repeated-exposure-to-media-images-of-traumatic-events-may-be-harmful-to-mental-and-physical-health.html [10 January 2015]

Auge, Marc. 1995. *Non-Places: Introduction to an Anthropology of Supermodernity*. London: Verso.

AVID. 1998. Technology glossary. Available from: http://resources.avid.com/SupportFiles/attach/MasterGlossary_4.0_8.0.pdf [10 January 2015]

Bachelard, Gaston. 1994. *The Poetics of Space* (trans. Maria Jolas). Boston: Beacon Press (original work published 1958).

Bacher, Lutz. 1978. *Die mobile Inszenierung: Eine kritische Analyse der langen Kamerabewegung im narrativen Film*. New York: Arno Press.

BachiRules. 2012. 9 month in 1000 pictures stop motion (Pregnancy time lapse!). [Video file]. Available from: http://www.youtube.com/watch?v=WbLpTgTZGsg [8 December 2013]

Bagel Head saline injections are new body art fad. *New York Daily News* [online]. 26 September. Available from: http://www.nydailynews.com/news/world/bagel-head-saline-injections-new-body-art-fad-article-1.1168711 [10 January 2015]

Baraniuk, Chris. 2013. Tyrannical loops: The inappropriateness of instant replay in the wake of destruction. *The Machine Starts* [online]. 16 April. Available from:

http://www.themachinestarts.com/read/2013-04-tyrannical-loops-inappropriateness-of-instant-replay-wake-destruction [15 January 2015].

Baraniuk, Chris. 2013. "The Wheel of the Devil": On Vine, gifs and the power of the loop. *The Machine Starts* [online]. January 2013. Available from: http://themachinestarts.com/read/2013-01-the-wheel-of-the-devil-vine-gifs-idea-of-loop [10 January 2015]

Barocas, S., Hood, S., and Ziewitz, M. 2013. Governing algorithms: A provocation piece. [Online]. Available from: http://governingalgorithms.org/resources/provocation-piece/ [9 January 2015]

Barthes, Roland. 1975. *The Pleasure of the Text*. Paris: Editions du Seuil.

Batman wins YouTube: Our top 10 most popular superheroes. 2013 [Online]. Available from: http://youtube-trends.blogspot.com/2013/08/batman-wins-youtube-our-top-10-most.html [15 August 2013]

Baudrillard, Jean. The violence of the image. [Online]. Available from: http://www.egs.edu/faculty/jean-baudrillard/articles/the-violence-of-the-image/ [10 January 2015]

BBC News. 2011. Artist forced to remove head camera implant. [Online]. Available from: http://www.bbc.co.uk/news/entertainment-arts-12429353 [10 January 2015]

BBC Worldwide. 2009. Real birds eye view! Golden Eagle in flight - Animal Camera – BBC. [Video file]. Available from: http://www.youtube.com/watch?v=lswBDZuL-8w [8 January 2015]

Beckett, Samuel. 1965. *The Unnameable, in Three Novels*. New York: Grove Press.

Bellour, Raymond. 2012. *Between-the-Images*. Zurich: Ringier.

Bellour, Raymond. 2012. Video Utopia. In: *Between-the-Images*. Zurich: Ringier.

Benjamin, Walter. 1973. *Charles Baudelaire: A Lyric Poet in the Era of High Capitalism*. London: New Left Books.

Berger, John. 1972. *Ways of Seeing*. New York: Penguin.

Berger, John. 1991. *About Looking*. New York: Vintage International.

Berkowitz, Joe. 2012. A dog's-eye view of music video directing. *Fast Company* [online]. 28 February. Available from:

http://www.fastcocreate.com/1680004/a-dogs-eye-view-of-music-video-directing [8 January 2015].

Bilal, Waafa. http://www.3rdi.me

Birnbaum, Daniel. 1999. Loop guru: Marijke van Warmerdam. *Frieze* [online]. 44 (January-February 1999). Available from: http://www.frieze.com/issue/article/loop_guru/ [10 January 2015]

Blast Theory. 2012. A machine to see with. [Online]. Available at: http://www.blasttheory.co.uk/projects/a-machine-to-see-with/ [7 December 2014].

Bliss, Rob, 2013, Homeless veteran time-lapse transformation. [Video file]. Available from: http://www.youtube.com/watch?v=6a6VVncgHcY [8 December 2013]

Bloom, Harald. 2003. *Thomas Pynchon*. London: Chelsea House.

Blue. N.d.. Blue: Music for the film by Derek Jarman. [Online]. Available at
http://www.answers.com/topic/blue-music-for-the-film-by-derek-jarman [26 July 2014].

Boehme, Gernot. 1993. Atmosphere as the fundamental concept of a new aesthetics. [Online]. Available from: http://desteceres.com/boehme.pdf [9 January 2015]

Boesel, Whitney Erin. 2013. Documenting tragedy: Vine and the Boston Marathon. *The Society Pages* [0nline]. 16 April. Available from: http://thesocietypages.org/cyborgology/2013/04/16/documenting-tragedy-vine-and-the-boston-marathon/ [15 January 2015]

Bordwell, David. 2002. Intensified continuity: Visual style in contemporary American film. *Film Quarterly*. 55 (3): 16-28. Available from: http://www.jstor.org/stable/1213701 [16 June 2010].

Borenstein, Greg. 2012. *Making Things See*. San Francisco: Maker Media.

Bosker, Bianca. 2014. Nice to meet you, I've already taken your picture. *Huffington Post* [online]. 2 October. Available from: http://www.huffingtonpost.com/2014/02/10/narrative-clip_n_4760580.html?1392058555

Bridle, James. 2011. Web Directions South. Closing Keynote (transcript). Available from: http://www.webdirections.org/resources/james-bridle-waving-at-the-machines/ [10 January 2015]

British Independent Film Awards. 2003. Lights, camera, action - Introducing the Nokia shorts. [Online]. 20 July 2003. Available from:

http://www.bifa.org.uk/releases/2003-nokia-announces-collaboration-with-british-independent-film-awards-and-raindance-film-festival [10 January 2015]

Burgess, Jean. 2009. YouTube: A short history of competing futures. In: Burgess & Green (eds.), *YouTube: Online Video and Participatory Culture*. Cambridge, UK: Polity Press. Available from: http://web.mit.edu/comm-forum/mit6/papers/Burgess.pdf [9 January 2015].

Burugorri, Marta. 2014. Trapped in repetition: reflections on GIFs and Peter Land. *Institute of Network Cultures* [online]. 30 January. Available from: http://networkcultures.org/videovortex/2014/01/30/trapped-in-repetition-reflections-on-gifs-and-peter-land/ [10 January 2015]

Cade, DL. 2014. Adam Magyar talks about the tech behind his mesmerizing photo and video series. *Petapixel* [online]. 13 January. Available from: http://petapixel.com/2014/01/13/adam-magyar-talks-tech-behind-mesmerizing-photo-video-series/ [8 January 2015]

Cade, DL. 2014. Google's new camera app takes a stand against the scourge that is vertical video. *Petapixel* [online]. 20 April 2014. http://petapixel.com/2014/04/20/googles-new-camera-app-takes-stand-scourge-vertical-video/ [10 January 2015]

Cade, DL. 2014. Slow motion aerial video takes you inside a fireworks show. *Petapixel* [online]. 22 April 2014. Available from: http://petapixel.com/2014/04/22/slow-motion-aerial-video-takes-inside-fireworks-show/ [8 January 2015]

Cage, John. 1937. *The Future of Music*. Available from: http://www.medienkunstnetz.de/source-text/41/ [10 January 2015]

Cain, Fraser. 2008. How can galaxies recede faster than the speed of light? *Universe Today* [online]. 30 January. Available at http://www.universetoday.com/13808/how-can-galaxies-recede-faster-than-the-speed-of-light/ [10 January 2015]

Campanelli, Vito. 2013. Video Vortex #9 conference, Lüneburg, Germany. Program available from: http://www.leuphana.de/fileadmin/user_upload/Forschungseinrichtungen/cdc/files/videovortex9_program.pdf

Certeau, M. de. 1984. *The Practice of Everyday Life* (trans. S. Rendall). Berkeley: University of California Press.

Cho, Eddie. 2013. Editor's review: Minecraft for Mac. *Download.com* [online]. 19 August. Available from: http://download.cnet.com/Minecraft/3000-2097_4-75980617.html#ixzz323YK0200

Cinemagraphs. N.d. The History of Cinemagraphs. [Online]. Available from: http://cinemagraphs.com/about/

Cioran, Emile. 1952. *All Gall Is divided: Gnomes and Apothegms* (trans. Richard Howard). New York: Arcade Publishing (original work published 1952). Available from: http://books.google.co.uk/books/about/All_Gall_is_Divided.html?id=LlLzGOEH7B4C [13 October 2013]

Class. 2011. *Tech Terms* [online]. Available from: http://www.techterms.com/definition/class [9 January 2015]

Cohen, Joshua. 2011. Cinemagraphs are animated gifs for adults. *Tubefilter* [online]. 10 July 2011. Available from: http://www.tubefilter.com/2011/07/10/cinemgraph/ [10 January 2015]

Coleman, Beth. 2013. Video Vortex 9 Lüneburg, 2013. Available from: http://networkcultures.org/wpmu/culturevortex/category/lueneburg/

Colner, Miha. 2011. Dan Oki: Generatio Aequivoca. [Online]. April 2011. Available from: http://www.kibla.org/en/sections/kibela-space-for-art/archive/kibela-arhiv/2011/dan-oki-generatio-aequivoca/

Cooper, W. E. 1985. Is art a form of life? *Dialogue*. 24 (3): 443-453.

Cortsen, Rikke Platz. 2012. *Comics as Assemblage: How spatio-temporality in comics is constructed*. Ph.D. thesis, Københavns Universitet, Humanistisk Fakultet.

Costello, Jane. 2014. Me, my son and Minecreaft. *Guardian* [online]. 8 March. Available from: http://www.theguardian.com/lifeandstyle/2014/mar/08/me-my-son-minecraft-blocks-game?CMP=twt_gu [10 January 2015]

Cox, Savannah. 2013. The most important image captured by Hubble. *All That Is Interesting* [online]. 5 September. Available at http://all-that-is-interesting.com/important-image-captured-by-hubble

Cubitt, S., D. Palmer, and L. Walkling. 2011. Reflections on medium specificity occasioned by the symposium 'Digital Light: Technique, Technology, Creation'. *Moving Image Review & Art Journal*. 1 (1) January 2012: 37.

D'Angelo, Mike. 2013. How Wong Kar-Wai turned 22 seconds into an eternity. *The Dissolve* [online]. 16 October 2013. Available from: http://thedissolve.com/features/movie-of-the-week/221-how-wong-kar-wai-turned-22-seconds-into-an-eternit/ [10 January 2015]

Danny MacAskill. 2014. Wikipedia article. [Online]. Available from: http://en.wikipedia.org/wiki/Danny_MacAskill [10 January 2015]

Dawes, Brandon. 2008. Cinema redux. Available from: http://brendandawes.com/projects/cinemaredux/

Davidson, Alex. 2014. Derek Jarman: Five essential films. *British Film Institute* [online]. 6 February. Available from: http://www.bfi.org.uk/news-opinion/news-bfi/lists/derek-jarman-five-essential-films [10 January 2015]

Deakins, Roger. 2008. Directors and technical question! [Online]. Available from: http://www.rogerdeakins.com/forum2/viewtopic.php?f=1&t=249

Deering, Marc. 2000. Show don't tell - a primer in sequential storytelling. *Pop Image* [online]. Available from: http://www.popimage.com/jan00/industrial/showtell.html

Desertmoondubai. 2012. Cinemagraphs – Wonderful living moments captured in a still shot. [Online]. Available from: http://desertmonsoondubai.com/2012/12/10/cinemagraphs-wonderful-living-moments-captured-in-a-still-shot/ [10 January 2015]

Diaz, Ann-Christine. 2014. Take 30 seconds to watch the winners of Tribeca Film Festival's Vine contest. *Advertising Age* [online]. 15 April. Available from: http://adage.com/article/creativity-news/watch-winners-tribeca-film-festival-s-vine-contest/292658/ [15 January 2015].

Die kleine Filmfabrik. 2012. Alexander Kluge: Das Handwerk des Erzählers. [Video file]. Available from: https://www.youtube.com/watch?v=medmyVcsMdo [8 January 2015]

DIY Drone Brigade. N.d. Facebook page. [Online]. Available from: https://www.facebook.com/DIYDB [27 February 2014]

Donald, James. 2003. Flannery. Botanising the interface. [Online]. Available from: http://www.icinema.unsw.edu.au/assets/161/flannery.pdf [9 January 2015].

Dziga Vertov. 2014. Wikipedia article. [Online]. http://en.wikipedia.org/wiki/Dziga_Vertov

Ebert, Robert. 1996. Chungking Express (review). [Online]. Available from: http://www.rogerebert.com/reviews/chungking-express-1996 [20 January 2015]

Echograph. N.d. See how to create a new visual story in a matter of minutes with Echograph. [Online]. Available from: http://echographs.com/creating/

Edmondson, Amy. 1987. A Fuller Explanation. Appendix E: Glossary. Available from: http://www.synearth.net/afullerex/145.htm [9 January 2015]

Eisenberg, Anne: When a camcorder becomes a life partner. *New York Times* [online]. 6 November 6. Available from: http://www.nytimes.com/2010/11/07/business/07novel.html?_r=0

Eisner, Will. 1985. *Comics and Sequential Art*. Florida: Poorhouse Press.

Elin, Larry. 2001. *Designing and Developing Multimedia: A Practical Guide for the Producer, Director, and Writer*. New York: Allyn & Bacon.

Elsaesser, Thomas. 2008. 'Constructive Instability'. Or: The life of things as the Cinema's Afterlife. In: Lovink, Niederer (ed.). *Video Vortex Reader I. Responses to YouTube* (13-32). Amsterdam: Institute of Network Cultures.

Emil Cioran. 2013. Wikipedia article.[Online]. Available at http://en.wikipedia.org/wiki/Emil_Cioran / [17 October 2013]

Faster-than-light. 2014. Wikipedia article. [Online]. http://en.wikipedia.org/wiki/Faster-than-light

Entfesselte Kamera. 2013. Wikipedia article. [Online]. http://de.wikipedia.org/wiki/Entfesselte_Kamera

Film Zeit. N.d. Karl Freund. [Online]. http://www.film-zeit.de/Person/11526/Karl-Freund/

Flip Video. 2014. Wikipedia article. [Online]. http://en.wikipedia.org/wiki/Flip_Video

Flock, Elizabeth. 2011. Cinemagraphs: What it looks like when a photo moves. *Washington Post* [online]. 8 July. Available from: http://www.washingtonpost.com/blogs/blogpost/post/cinemagraphs-what-it-looks-like-when-a-photo-moves/2011/07/08/gIQAONez3H_blog.html [15 January 2015]

Flusser, Vilem. 1983. Imagination. [Online]. Available from: http://slaag.files.wordpress.com/2011/12/flusser_imagination.pdf [10 January 2015]

Flusser, Vilem. 1990. Flusser's view on art. *Artforum* 29 (4): 25-27. Available from: https://s3.amazonaws.com/arena-attachments/151303/856a06a1ba540f1c75ae58d09e52c8a5.pdf [10 January 2015]

Flusser, Vilem. 1995. Andreas Müller-Pohle. In: M.M. Evans & A. Hopkinson (eds.), *Contemporary Photographers* (806). Detroit: St. James Press. Available at http://www.muellerpohle.net/texts/essays/flusseramp1.html

Flusser, Vilem. 2002. The future of writing. In *Writings* (trans. Andreas Ströhl). Minneapolis: University of Minnesota Press.

Flusser, Vilém. N.d. *The Future of Writing* (trans. Erik Eisel). 1983-84. Available from: http://www.egs.edu/library/vilem-flusser/quotes/ [10 January 2015].

Gibson, William. 1984. *Neuromancer*. New York: Ace.

GIFGIF. 2014. Which better expresses excitement? MIT Project. Available from: http://gifgif.media.mit.edu [15 January 2015]:

Gillespie, Tarleton. **2012**. Can an algorithm be wrong? *Limn* [online]. Issue 2: Crowds and Clouds. Available from: http://limn.it/can-an-algorithm-be-wrong/ [9 January 2015]

Glove and Boots. 2013. Vertical Video Syndrome – A PSA. [Video file]. Available at https://www.youtube.com/watch?v=Bt9zSfinwFA

Goldberg, David. 2002. EnterFrame: Cage, Deleuze and Macromedia Director. *Afterimage* 30 (1) July-August 2002.

Google Search Trends. Available from: http://www.google.com/trends/explore?hl=en-US#q=vertical+video+syndrome&cmpt=q

GoPro. 2013a. GoPro: Backflip Over 72ft Canyon - Kelly McGarry Red Bull Rampage 2013. [Video file]. Available from: https://www.youtube.com/watch?v=x76VEPXYaI0 [21 February 2014]

GoPro. 2013b. GoPro: Fireman Saves Kitten . 2013. Available from: http://www.youtube.com/watch?v=CjB_oVeq8Lo [8 January 2015]

GoPro. 2014. Wikipedia article. [Online]. Available from: http://en.wikipedia.org/wiki/GoPro [10 January 2015]

Green, Barry. Sensor artifacts and CMOS rolling shutter. *DVX User* [online]. Available from: http://dvxuser.com/jason/CMOS-CCD/

Green, Joshua. 2009. Mapping YouTube's common culture. In: Jean Burgess & Joshua Green (eds.), *YouTube: Online Video and Participatory Culture*. New York: Polity Press.

Greenaway, Peter. 2003. Cinema Militans lecture at the Dutch Film Festival. Available from: http://petergreenaway.org.uk/essay3.htm

HAIP2012. 2012. Designing the archive user interface: Robert Ochshorn, interlace/montage interdit. Video file. Available from: http://www.youtube.com/watch?v=2Wwa8zewDbc [8 January 2015]

Hamid, Rahul. 2004. Der Letzte Mann (The Last Laugh). *Senses of Cinema* [online]. Available from: http://sensesofcinema.com/2004/cteq/der_letzte_mann/ [10 January 2015]

Hammer, Joshua. 2014. Einstein's camera. How one renegade photographer is hacking the concept of time. *Medium* [online]. Available from: https://medium.com/matter/88aa8a185898

Hancock, Hugh. 2014. Minecraft, the Sims, and the future of filmmaking. *The Antipope* [online]. Available from: http://www.antipope.org/charlie/blog-static/2014/02/minecraft-the-sims-and-the-fut.html [10 January 2015]

Hedges, Chris. 2009. *Empire of Illusions, The End of Literacy and the Triumph of Spectacle*. New York: Nation Books.

Helmond, Anne. 2011. Video Vortex: Florian Cramer "Bokeh is a form of visual fetishism, it is not avant-garde but porn." [Blog]. Available from: http://www.simonwyndham.co.uk/bokeh-porn.html [10 January 2015]

Hillis, Danny. 1998. *The Pattern in the Stone*. Quoted in: Murray, Janet. Inventing the medium. NINCH Building Blocks Workshop October 2000. Available from: http://www.ninch.org/bb/report/JM2.pdf [10 January 2015]

Hochman, Nadav, and Lev Manovich. 2013. Zooming into an Instagram City: Reading the local through social media. *First Monday* 18 (7). Available from: http://firstmonday.org/ojs/index.php/fm/article/view/4711/3698 [9 January 2015]

Frans Hofmeester, 2013. Birth to 13 years in 3 min. 30 sec. Time Lapse Lotte. (The Original). [Video file]. Available from: http://www.youtube.com/watch?v=nN_jcom8TR4 [8 December 2013]

Holschbach, Susanne. 2010. Framing [on] Flickr: Modes of channeling an indisciplinary reservoir of images. *PhotoResearcher*, 14: 46–53.

Hooper, Riley. 2012. Easy Vimeo projects. [Video file]. Available from: http://vimeo.com/videoschool/lesson/167/easy-vimeo-projects [8 January 2015]

Ilnitzky, Ula. 2011. Wafaa Bilal, NYU artist, gets camera implanted in head. *Huffington Post* [online]. 23 November. Available from: http://www.huffingtonpost.com/2010/11/23/wafaa-bilal-nyu-artist-ge_n_787446.html [10 January 2015].

IndieReign. 2013. Filmmakers, make use of new, Vine app! *Indie Reign* [blog]. Available from: http://blog.indiereign.com/feature-article-filmmakers-make-use-of-filmmaking-app-vine/ [15 January 2015]

Inge, Sophie. 2013. VIDEO: Eagle-cam offers bird's eye view of Alps. *The Local* [online]. 18 September. Available from: http://www.thelocal.fr/20130918/video-viewers-blown-away-by-birds-eye-view-of-chamonix [8 January 2015]

Inspired Bicycles. 2009. Danny MacAskill April 2009. [Video file]. Available from: http://www.youtube.com/watch?v=Z19zFlPah-o [10 January 2015]

Iordanova, Diana. 2013. Digital disruption: Cinema moves online (speech), Department of Cinema and Digital Media, Izmir University of Economics, May 2013. Available from: http://www.st-andrews.ac.uk/filmstudies/dina-iordanova-travels-to-turkey/ and http://vcd-ieu.tumblr.com/post/51461708835/dina-iordanova-digital-disruption-cinema-moves

Irony. 2014. Wikipedia article. [Online]. Available from: en.wikipedia.org/wiki/irony

Jarman, Derek. 1993. Blue (film).

jMax home page. N.d. http://jmax.sourceforge.net

Jurek, Thom. N.d. Blue: A Film by Derek Jarman. *AllMusic* (online). Available from: http://www.allmusic.com/album/blue-a-film-by-derek-jarman-mw0000114044 [5 December 2014].

Jurgensen, John. 2013. Netflix says binge viewing is no 'House of Cards': Half the users it studied watch an entire season in one week. *Wall Street Journal* [online]. Available from: http://online.wsj.com/news/articles/SB10001424052702303932504579254031017586624 [9 January 2015]

Jurgenson, Nathan. 2013a. Documentary oversaturation. *The Society Pages* [online]. 28 January. Available from: http://thesocietypages.org/cyborgology/2013/01/28/documentary-oversaturation/

Jurgenson, Nathan. 2013b. Vine, Vinepeek, and visual efficiency. *The Society Pages* [online]. 27 January. Available from: http://thesocietypages.org/cyborgology/2013/01/27/vine-vinepeek-and-visual-efficiency/ [10 January 2015]

Kato, Shuson. N.d. Untitled haiku. Available from: http://www.haikusociety.com/14 [9 January 2015]

Kenny, Glenn. 2008. Criterion's first Blu-Ray: "Chungking Express". *Same Came Running* [blog]. 28 November. Available from: http://somecamerunning.typepad.com/some_came_running/2008/11/criterions-first-bluray-chungking-express.html [8 January 2015]

Kesenne, Sarah. 2011. On Gig Flix. In: Geert Lovink & Rachel Somers Miles (eds). *Video Vortex Reader II: Moving Images beyond YouTube*. Amsterdam: Institute of Network Cultures.

Kipphoff, Petra. 2007. Coincidence and illumination. Gerhard Richter's stained glass window opens a new chapter in the long career of the Cologne Cathedral. *Sight and Sight* [online]. Available from: http://signandsight.com/features/1547.html [10 May 2014].

Kracauer, Siegfried. 1947. *From Caligari to Hitler*. Available from: http://www.menggang.com/book/02/caligarihitler/caligarihitler.txt

Lanier, Jaron. 2010. *You Are Not a Gadget: A Manifesto*. New York: Alfred A. Knopf.

Lasky, Michael. 2014. Narrative Clip. Wearable camera records your life at two shots per minute. *Wired* [online]. 13 February. Available from: http://www.wired.com/reviews/2014/02/narrative-clip/ [10 January 2015]

Laurel, Brenda. 1993. *Computers as Theatre*. New York: Addison-Wesley.

Lazzarato, Maurizio. 2007. Video, flows and real time. In: *Video Philosophy*. Available from: http://m.friendfeedmedia.com/8ced04759aedb137c74d00a07f7f10165d592d02 [15 January 2015]

Lee, Edward. 2010. Camille Utterback and the technology of interactive art. *Huffington Post* [online]. Available from: http://www.huffingtonpost.com/edward-lee/camille-utterback-and-the_b_775070.html

LEGO Group. 2011. A short presentation. Available from: http://cache.lego.com/upload/contentTemplating/AboutUsFactsAndFiguresContent/otherfiles/downloadC60A8E1ACF6EEDBEFB62747F119FBDC6.pdf [5 December 2014]

Levin, Golan. 2005. An informal catalogue of slit-scan video artworks and research. Available from: http://www.flong.com/texts/lists/slit_scan/

Life+Times, 2011. Pregame 05.27.2011. [Video file]. Available at http://lifeandtimes.com/pregame

Loew, Matthew. 2013. Why playing with LEGO® is so important! *Engineering* [online]. 13 December. Available from: http://www.engineering.com/DesignSoftware/DesignSoftwareArticles/ArticleID/6815/Why-Playing-with-LEGO-is-so-Important.aspx [5 December 2014].

Lovink, Geert and Niederer, Sabine (eds.). 2008. *Video Vortex Reader I*. Amsterdam: Institute of Network Cultures.

Lovink, Geert and Rachel Somers Miles (eds). 2011. *Video Vortex Reader II: Moving Images beyond YouTube*. Amsterdam: Institute of Network Cultures.

Lushetich, Natasha. 2007. *Blast Theory: The Politics and Aesthetics of Interactivity*. Dissertation towards the degree of Master of Arts. University of Exter. Available from: http://www.blasttheory.co.uk/bt/documents/Blast_Theory_The_Politics_and_Aesthetics_of_Interactivity.pdf [9 January 2015].

Madrigal, Alexis C. 2013. Bjork explaining television is everything you'd imagine Bjork explaining television to be. *The Atlantic* [online]. Available from: http://www.theatlantic.com/technology/archive/2013/11/bjork-explaining-television-is-everything-youd-imagine-bjork-explaining-television-to-be/281589/ [9 January 2015]

Magyar, Adam. 2011. Adam Magyar - Stainless, Alexanderplatz. [Video file]. Available from: http://vimeo.com/83663312 [8 January 2015]

Magyar, Adam. Photos of time. [Video file]. Available from: http://vimeo.com/78667444 [8 January 2015].

Manovich, Lev. 2001. *The Language of New Media*. Boston: MIT Press.

Manovich, Lev. 2012. Media after software. Available from: http://lab.softwarestudies.com/2012/11/new-article-by-lev-manovich-media-after.html [10 January 2015}

Manovich, Lev. 2013. Instagram Cities: ImagePlot, project Phototrails. Available from: http://flowingdata.com/2013/07/03/instagram-cities/ [4 July 2013]

Massumi, Brian. 2002. *Parables for the Virtual: Movement, Affect, Sensation*. Durham: Duke University Press.

Matteucci, Giovanni. 2013. Towards a Wittgensteinian aesthetics: Wollheim and the analysis of aesthetic practices. *Aisthesis; Pratiche, linguaggi e saperi dell'estetico* 6 (1): 67-83. Available from: http://www.fupress.net/index.php/aisthesis/article/view/12838/12160. [9 Jan. 2015]

Max (software). 2014. Wikipedia article. [Online]. Available from: http://en.wikipedia.org/wiki/Max_(software)

McCarthy, Anna. 2001. *Ambient Television: Visual Culture and Public Space*. Durham: Duke University Press.

Media Art Net. N.d. Jeffrey Shaw: The Legible City. Available from: http://www.medienkunstnetz.de/works/the-legible-city/ [5 January 2015].

Menard, David George. 2009. Bazinian Theory - Toward a synthesis of cinema - a theory of the long take moving camera. Available from: http://www.horschamp.qc.ca/new_offscreen/synthesis_theory.html

Metz, Christian. 1974, *Language and Cinema*. The Hague: Mouton & Co.

Miles, Adrian. 2013. The First Quarter. Available at http://vogmae.net.au/works/2013/firstquarter/ [10 January 2015]

Miller, Michael. 2010. *SAMS Teach Yourself You Tube in 10 Minutes*. Carmel, IN: SAMS Publishing.

Miller, Shannon. 2010. Branded Tipp-Experience pushes YouTube interactivity. Available from: *GigaOM* [online]. Available from: http://gigaom.com/2010/10/07/branded-tipp-experience-pushes-youtubes-interactivity/ [10 January 2015]

Miller Hocking, Sherry. 2013. A brief look at analog imaging instruments. *Televisions Project* [online]. Available from: http://televisionsproject.org/a-brief-look-at-analog-imaging-instruments/ [28.11.14]

Monaco, James. 2009. *How to Read a Film* (4th ed.). Oxford: Oxford University Press.

Moran, Lee. 2014. See it: Camera falls from skydiving airplane and lands in pigpen. *New York Daily News* [online]. 12 February 12. Available from: http://www.nydailynews.com/news/national/camera-falls-airplane-lands-pigpen-article-1.1610971#ixzz2uHEayvBS [24 February 2014].

MovingWeb. 2011. What is web video? The survey! Available from: http://www.movingweb.org/2011/07/07/what-is-web-video-the-survey/ [29 October 2014].

Negarestani, Reza. 2008. *Cyclonopedia: Complicity with Anonymous*. Melbourne: Re-Press.

Network Cultures. 2013. Society of the Query #1 - Lev Manovich. [Video file]. Available from: http://vimeo.com/81484988 [9 January 2015]

Neves, Joshua 2013, Video Theory. Video Vortex #009. Available at: http://vimeo.com/66055799

Noise (video). Wikipedia article. [Online]. Available from: http://en.wikipedia.org/wiki/Noise_(video) [5 December 2014].

Nolan, Jonathan (creator). 2011. *Person of Interest* (television program). Season 1, episode 1, 22 September.

Ochshorn, M.2012. Compression. Available from: http://rmozone.com/compression/opening_week/ [10 January 2015]

Pamuk, Orhan. 2001. *My Name Is Red*. London: Faber and Faber.

Parikka, Jussi. 2013. Dust and exhaustion: The labor of media materialism. *CTheory* [online]. Available from: http://www.ctheory.net/articles.aspx?id=726 [10 January 2015]

Pew Research Center. 2013. Online video 2013. Available from: http://pewinternet.org/~/media/Files/Reports/2013/PIP_Online%20Video%202013.pdf [12 October 2013]

Pfeiffer, Sylvia. 2010. *The Definitive Guide to HTML5 Video*. New York: Apress.

Phillips, Baxter. 1988. *Cut: The Unseen Cinema*. New York: Random House.

Processing (programming language). 2014. Wikipedia article. [Online]. Available from: http://en.wikipedia.org/wiki/Processing_(programming_language)

Processing home page. N.d. http://processing.org

Pynchon, Thomas. 1966. *The Crying of Lot 49*. New York: Lippincott.

RE: Assemblies of Video. 2013. Video Vortex #9 Conference, Lüneburg, Germany. Available from: http://cdc.leuphana.com/structure/moving-image-lab/video-vortex-9/ [9 January 2015].

Red Bull. 2013. Danny MacAskill's Imaginate. [Video file]. Available from: https://www.youtube.com/watch?v=Sv3xVOs7_No [8 January 2015].

Rehage, Christoph. 2009. The Longest Way 1.0 - walk through China and grow a beard! - a photo every day timelapse. [Video file]. Available from; http://www.youtube.com/watch?v=5ky6vgQfU24 [8 January 2015].

Röscheisen, Thilo. 2013. It's the creative, stupid! *Drama Blog* [blog]. Available from: http://drama-blog.de/its-the-creative-stupid/ [25 August 2013].

Rohrer, Finlo. 2013. Vine: Six things people have learned about six-second video in a week. *BBC News* [online]. Available from: http://www.bbc.co.uk/news/magazine-21267741 [31 January 2013].

Rojas, Natalia. N.d. The Faces of Facebook. Available from: http://app.thefacesoffacebook.com

Rosenbaum, Jonathan. 1995. Godard in the age of video [SOFT AND HARD]. *Chicago Reader*, 17 November. Available at: http://www.jonathanrosenbaum.net/1995/11/godard-in-the-age-of-video/ [7 December 2014]

Rouse, Margaret. 2005. Dynamic and static. *Tech Target* [online]. Available from: http://searchnetworking.techtarget.com/definition/dynamic-and-static [5 Dezember 2014]

Sadoul, Georges. 1982. *Geschichte der Filmkunst*. Frankfurt, Germany: Fischer Taschenbuch.

Salvia, Peter. 2010. The foundry fixing rolling shutter. *Pro-Active-Ly* [blog]. 1 June. Available from: https://petersalvia.wordpress.com/tag/how-to-fix-canon-5d-mark-ii-rolling-shutter/ [10 January 2015]

Schneider, Florian. Wohin kann das Dokumentarische flüchten? Von neuen Wegen in eine neue Wirklichkeit. Available from: http://berlinergazette.de/dokumentarische-neue-wirklichkeit/

Scopitone. 2014. Wikipedia article. [Online]. Available from: http://en.wikipedia.org/wiki/Scopitone

Seaver, Nick. 2012. Algorithmic recommendations and synaptic functions. *Limn* [online]. Issue 2: *Crowds and Clouds*. Available from: http://limn.it/algorithmic-recommendations-and-synaptic-functions/ [9 January 2015]

Serres, Michel. 1995. *Genesis* (trans. G. J. a. J. Nielson). Ann Arbor: University of Michigan Press.

Sherman, Tom. 2008. The nine lives of video art: Technological evolution, the repeated near-death of video art, and the life force of vernacular video. Available at: http://www.gama-gateway.eu/uploads/media/Nine_lives_of_video_art.pdf

Stableford, Dylan. 2012. Felix Baumgartner's space jump captivates internet, Twitter. *Yahoo News* [online]. Available from: http://news.yahoo.com/blogs/lookout/felix-baumgartner-space-jump-captivates-internet-twitter-191838284.html

Stanjek, Klaus. 1987. Kamerabewegungen: Gestaltungstile verschiedener Regisseure, Seminar HFF Munich. (lecture notes by author)

Stelarc. 2014. Wikipedia article. [Online]. Available from: http://en.wikipedia.org/wiki/Stelarc

Stephenson, Neal. 1999. In the beginning ... Was the command line. Available from: http://www.cryptonomicon.com/beginning.html

Steiner, Dietmar. N.d. Benutzeroberfläche Stadt. The city as user interface. Available from: http://www.wien.gv.at/stadtentwicklung/studien/pdf/b006822.pdf [12 November 2014]

Stiegler, Bernhard. 2010. *Technics and Time 3 – Cinematic Time and the Question of Malaise*. Stanford, CA: Stanford University Press.

Surveillance cinema. 2010. *Cinemaelectronica* [Blog]. 1 March. Available from: http://cinemaelectronica.wordpress.com/2010/03/01/surveillance-cinema/ [9 January 2015]

SxSW. 2012. The New Aesthetic: Seeing Like Digital Devices. Available from: http://schedule.sxsw.com/2012/events/event_IAP11102 [10 January 2015]

Thumber. N.d. Watch a movie at a glance. Available from: http://www.threewordtitle.com/thumber/

TippEx. 2010. A Hunter ____ a Bear. [Video file]. Available at http://www.youtube.com/user/tippexperience

TippEx. 2012. TippExperience 2. [Video file]. Available at http://www.thinkwithgoogle.com/campaigns/tippex-tippexperience-2.html

Tobias, Scott. 2008. The Last Laugh (DVD Review). *A.V. Club* [online]. 2 September. Available from: http://www.avclub.com/articles/the-last-laugh,6874/ [10 January 2015]

Treske, Andreas. 2013. *The Inner Life of Video Spheres*. Amsterdam: Institute of Network Cultures.

Turvey, Malcolm. 2010. Arnheim and Modernism. In: Scott Higgins (ed.), *Arnheim for Film and Media Studies*. London: Routledge.

Uexküll, Jakob von. 2010. *A Foray into the Worlds of Animals and Humans. With a Theory of Meaning* (trans. Joseph D. O'Neil). Minneapolis: University of Minnesota Press.

Ulucan, Ege. 2013. Static. [Video file]. Available at http://vimeo.com/79024700 [12 February 2014]

Urban Dictionary. n.d. Static. [Online] Available from: http://www.urbandictionary.com/define.php?term=static [5 December 2014].

Utterback, Camille. 2000–2002. Liquid Time. Available from: http://camilleutterback.com/projects/liquid-time-series/

Valdivia Bruch, Katerina. 2013. Two Singaporean artists in Berlin | Donna Ong | Part II. *Culture 360* [online]. 29 August. Available from: http://culture360.asef.org/magazine/two-singaporean-artists-in-berlin-donna-ong-part-ii/ [9 January 2015].

Vattimo, Gianni. 1992. *The Transparent Society*. Cambridge: Polity Press.

Vertical Cinema. N.d. About. Available from: http://verticalcinema.org/about/

Vertov, Dziga. 1985. *Kino-eye: The Writings of Dziga Vertov*. Berkeley: University of California Press.

Video in Max/MSP/Jitter. 2009. Available from: http://yin.arts.uci.edu/~studio/resources/prog09/video-jitter.pdf [10 January 2015]

Video synthesizer. 2014. Wikipedia article. [Online]. http://en.wikipedia.org/wiki/Video_synthesizer [10 January 2015].

Vine (software). 2014. Wikipedia article. [Online]. Available from: http://en.wikipedia.org/wiki/Vine_(software) [7 September 2013].

Vine Fenomenleri. (Vine Phenomens). 2013. Announcement of the student media club from Izmir University of Economics Available from: http://iletisim.ieu.edu.tr/medyakulubu/?p=538 [5 December 2014].

Warren, Christina. 2011. RIP Flip video camera. *Mashable* [online]. 12 April. Available from: http://mashable.com/2011/04/12/rip-flip-camera/ [10 January 2015].

Wasik, Bill. 2013. Why wearable tech will be as big as the smartphone. *Wired* [online]. Available from: http://www.wired.com/gadgetlab/2013/12/wearable-computers/all/ [10 January 2015]

Watt, James. 2013. The suppression of vertical videos. [Blog]. Available from: http://jameswatt.me/2013/02/09/the-suppression-of-vertical-videos/

Weber, Samuel. 1996. *Mass Mediauras: Form, Technics, Media*. Stanford, CA: Stanford University Press.

Weihsmann, Helmut. 1994. Virtuelle Raeume. In: Die Metaphysik des Dekors. Schriften der F.W. Murnau-Gesellschaft Wiesbaden Bd. 3. Marburg.

Wittgenstein and Wollheim: Seeing-As and Seeing-In. 2013. Conference at The Philosophy Division, University of Vienna. Program available from: http://philevents.org/event/show/12513 [5 January 2015]

Wortham, Jenna. 2013. Instagram video and the death of fantasy. *New York Times Bits* [online]. 24 June. Available from: http://bits.blogs.nytimes.com/2013/06/24/digital-diary-instagram-video-and-death-of-fantasy/ [10 January 2015].

Wyndham, Simon. 2010. Bokeh porn. *DV User* [online]. 18 October. Available at http://www.dvuser.co.uk/content.php?CID=245 [10 January 2015].

YouTube. 2014. Statistics. Available from: http://www.youtube.com/yt/press/statistics.html [7 February 2014]

YouTube. N.d. Trends Map. Available from:
http://www.youtube.com/trendsmap [5 January 2015]
YouTube Trends. Available from: http://youtube-trends.blogspot.com [15 August 2013,]
Zappile, Alex. 2012. Lets get vertical. [Video file]. Available from: https://vimeo.com/35266930 [8 January 2015]
Zielinski, Siegfried. 2014. Flusser, Vilem. Introduction II. A brief introduction to his media philosophy. Available from: http://www.flusser-archive.org/public/uploads/archive/projects/mecad/pdfs/introduction_II.A_brief_introduction_to_his_media_philosophy.pdf [10 January 2015]